Praise for ... Money

"Reading Phil Callaway is like playing in holy sand. You're having so much fun, you don't realize how much has gone into your shoes and is now sticking to your life."

Chris Fabry
author and host of *Chris Fabry Live*

"It is impossible to read this book without being changed. Changed in our demands, our expectations, and our level of contentment. If you struggle to balance the stuff of earth with the demands of heaven, or if you long for a lightning bolt of joy, this is just the ticket."

Sigmund Brouwer
author of *Broken Angel* and *The Last Disciple*

"If laughter is good for the soul, then Phil Callaway's new book is doubly good, for it administers not only a healthy dose of humor but also many beneficial spiritual lessons. If you wish to smile your way to contemplative thinking, read *Making Life Rich Without Any Money.*"

Janette Oke
bestselling author

"Once again, Phil Callaway has touched a nerve that hits all too close to home. This book is must-reading for anyone who wonders, *When is enough, enough?*"

Mike Yorkey
author of the Every Man's series

"Phil Callaway, one of the funniest and most profound humorists alive, has done it again! This time he reminds us of what's truly important. If the hustle-bustle of today's world has caused you to mix up your priorities hoping to get ahead, read this book. It'll make you laugh, make you think, maybe even make you cry. Most importantly, it will remind you (despite what your accountant says) how truly rich you already are."

Martha Bolton
writer for Bob Hope
coauthor of *It's Always Darkest Before the Fridge Door Opens*

"If the richest things in life are free, then Phil Callaway has a corner on the free market. Without trumpeting itself as such, this book is nourishment for the soul. It doesn't beat us over the head for our bad choices but rather provides us with a longing for good ones. This book is a pleasant journey, fun to read and meat for the soul."

John Fischer
author of *Fearless Faith*

"This book is a winner. From its heartwarming stories to its crystal clear message of simplicity, *Making Life Rich Without Any Money* will leave you challenged, changed, and chuckling. Don't just buy a copy of this book. Buy a dozen for your friends and family—and try to get a discount!"

Joel A. Freeman
NBA chaplain
author of *If Nobody Loves You, Create the Demand*

"In the middle of a very busy day, I began to skim this book. I was soon lost in laughter and wistful envy, and then encouraged that I can get off the treadmill of success and start enjoying *real* wealth. If you have ever wished for a more simple, more fulfilling life, read this book."

Ken Davis
motivational speaker and author

"Reading Phil Callaway is one of life's purest pleasures."

Ellen Vaughn
New York Times bestselling author

"I love Phil Callaway because he manages to accomplish what few writers can—masterfully blending laughter with learning."

Lee Strobel
author of *The Case for Faith*

"Phil Callaway is master of the funnybone and the heart-tug."

Mark Buchanan
author of *The Rest of God*

"I don't know of anyone else who make me laugh out loud, and then within moments, finds a way to touch the deep parts of my heart."

Steve Green
Dove Award–winning musical artist and author

Making Life Rich Without Any Money

PHIL CALLAWAY

HARVEST HOUSE PUBLISHERS
EUGENE, OREGON

Unless otherwise indicated, all Scripture quotations are taken from the HOLY BIBLE, NEW INTERNATIONAL VERSION®. NIV®. Copyright © 1973, 1978, 1984 by the International Bible Society. Used by permission of Zondervan. All rights reserved.

Verses marked NLT are taken from the *Holy Bible,* New Living Translation, copyright © 1996, 2004. Used by permission of Tyndale House Publishers, Inc., Wheaton, IL 60189 USA. All rights reserved.

Cover by Dan Pitts, Eagan, Minnesota

Cover photo © Sandy Jones / iStockphoto

MAKING LIFE RICH WITHOUT ANY MONEY
Copyright © 1998 by Phil Callaway
Published by Harvest House Publishers
Eugene, Oregon 97402
www.harvesthousepublishers.com

ISBN 978-0-7369-2631-7

The Library of Congress has cataloged the edition as follows:
Callaway, Phil, 1961–
Making life rich without any money / Phil Callaway
p. cm.
Includes bibliographical references.
ISBN 978-0-7369-0924-2
1. Success—Religious aspects—Christianity. 2. Christian life—Humor. 3. Callaway, Phil, 1961– I. Title.
BV4598.3.C35 1998
248.4—dc21 98-15498
CIP

Printed in the United States of America

09 10 11 12 13 14 15 16 17 / VP-NI / 10 9 8 7 6 5 4 3 2 1

For Dave, Dan, Tim, and Ruth.
From your rich little brother.
And for Andy, who asked.

Acknowledgments

When it comes to thanking people, I feel like a mosquito in a nudist colony. There's so much to do, I don't know where to start. But let me try.

My best friend, Ramona. A truly rich man is one whose wife runs into his arms when his hands are empty. You've done so these 27 years. Your love, faithfulness, and offspring have made me a wealthy man. I was born August 21, 1976—the day I met you.

The hundreds who answered my question "What has made your life rich?" Your much-appreciated insights on the lifestyles of the rich and not-so-famous were an inspiration. I wanted to pay you. Until I remembered the title of this book.

For wonderful answers to my questions and for enriching my life with your words and music: Max Lucado, Rick Warren, Michael W. Smith, Jim Cymbala, Gloria Gaither, Michael Card, Elisabeth Elliot, Steve Green, Twila Paris, Josh McDowell, Luis Palau, Larry Crabb, and Tony Campolo.

The Harvest House family. Bob Hawkins, Jr., a true believer; Gene Skinner, a first-rate editor; and Terry Glaspey, a top-notch encourager and a man of integrity—even on the golf course. Thanks, you three, for believing in this project all these years.

Vance Neudorf. For allowing me the freedom to be your imperfect friend. For walking with me through the shadows, celebrating with me in the light, and always pointing me higher. (PS. I'm still sorry about the lawn mower.)

My parents. Misers aren't much fun to live with, but they make wonderful ancestors. Thanks for the best inheritance a guy could wish for.

And finally, to you, the reader. Thanks for entrusting me with your valuable time. I trust the message of this book will enrich your life and help you smile a little too.

Contents

Money has never yet made anyone rich.

Lucius Annaeus Seneca (c. 4 BC–AD 65)

Preface: Poor Little Rich Boy

Something fabulous took place on the Callaway family tree one December: My parents celebrated their fifty-fifth wedding anniversary. As you know, a fifty-fifth anniversary is as rare these days as my Scottish cousins checking into the Ritz-Carlton, so we blew up balloons, bought gifts, combed the grandkids' hair, and ordered Hawaiian pizza. Then we bought space in a city newspaper and placed these words beside a picture of the well-weathered couple:

Happy fifty-fifth wedding anniversary!
From the five of us
awaiting our inheritance.

Those who knew my parents laughed quite heartily when they saw this. But not everyone joined them. When my older brother delivered the ad to the paper, the lady in charge of the classifieds hiked her eyebrows up to her hairline and slowly exhaled, "You sure you wanna say this? Won't it start a family feud or something?"

She had good reason. Never has a generation had more stuff to fight over. In fact, baby boomers are in the midst of a windfall inheritance of $6.8 trillion, meaning we'll soon be the wealthiest generation to ever enter a nursing home.[1] But we Callaway kids won't have much to feud about. Our parents spent their entire lives below what the government calls "the poverty line." When Mom and Dad pass through heaven's gates they will leave behind no stocks and bonds, just a few sticks of furniture and an old bomb of a car that sometimes runs.

I wasn't always thankful for this. Few children grow up coveting abject poverty. As a five-year-old, I stood before the sink, two pennies in hand, and discovered to my surprise that by simply holding the coins in front of a mirror I could double my assets. *If only I could make money this quickly,* I thought, and then I prayed out loud, "God, please make me rich."

But God didn't seem to hear.

In those days, my father's monthly income was $230—barely enough to buy sugar for my cereal. We were so poor, I thought everyone made meatloaf with wieners. It's safe to say that the buck stopped before it got to our house. As a result, we had no television. No skateboards. No insurance. In fact, we couldn't even afford a phone. One night I overheard Dad say to Mom, "Honey, we have enough money to last us the rest of our lives—unless we live past Thursday."

Thursday came and went, and the years slipped on by. Then, ever so slowly, it began to dawn on me that my prayer had been answered. Not in the way I hoped it would be, but in a far better way. At the age of 14, I still hadn't smelled the inside of a new car, savored a Big Mac, or slipped on a brand-new pair of jeans. I still hadn't tasted airplane omelet, experienced room service, or sipped Won Ton soup. But I had a backyard to run in, friends to play with, a dog that licked my face, parents who loved me, and the sneaking suspicion that God loved me too.

Through the years I have watched my fellow North Americans pursue wealth in all the wrong places. Just this morning I did a quick search on the Internet and discovered almost 2.5 million websites on how to get rich quick. (I even found out how to "earn $2000 a day for an hour's work," but according to my research, it doesn't work.)

Sadly, until the first edition of this book was published, I couldn't find one website on making life rich.

Yet when it comes right down to it, that's what we're all looking for, isn't it? Our TV promises that a newer car, a colder drink, or a cuter wife will be just the ticket. The billboards assure us that a step up the ladder, a plane ride to someplace exotic, or a worry-free journey to a Freedom 55 retirement will make our lives richer. But deep down, we know that money falls short.

If money made us happy, we'd be the happiest culture in history. Instead, we access more psychologists, lawyers, and antidepressants than any other people at any other time in history.

If money healed old wounds, ABBA would be back together, playing to packed-out stadiums. But when the Swedish supergroup was offered $1 billion to reunite and tour, Bjorn Ulvaeus, one of the four, said, "When you divide it by four, it's only $250 million per person."

If money gave us peace, billionaire Ted Turner would have no worries. But he told an interviewer, "I don't know if I have enough. I've lost tens of millions...who knows how much enough is."

At a commencement speech for Vassar College, horror writer Stephen King startled his audience with the scary truth:

> A couple of years ago I found out what "you can't take it with you" means. I found [that] out while I was lying in a ditch at the side of a country road, covered with mud and blood and with the tibia of my right leg poking out the side of my jeans like a branch of a tree taken down in a thunderstorm. I had a MasterCard in my wallet, but when you're lying in a ditch with broken glass in your hair, no one accepts MasterCard.
>
> We all know that life is ephemeral, but on that particular day and in the months that followed, I got a painful but extremely valuable look at life's simple backstage truths. We come in naked and broke. We may be dressed when we go out, but we're just as broke. Warren Buffet? Going to go out broke. Bill Gates? Going out broke. Tom Hanks? Going out broke. Steve King? Broke. Not a crying dime.
>
> All the money you earn, all the stocks you buy, all the mutual funds you trade—all of that is mostly smoke and

> mirrors. It's still going to be a quarter-past getting late whether you tell the time on a Timex or a Rolex. No matter how large your bank account, no matter how many credit cards you have, sooner or later things will begin to go wrong with the only three things you have that you can really call your own: your body, your spirit, and your mind. So I want you to consider making your life one long gift to others. And why not? All you have is on loan anyway. All that lasts is what you pass on.

I too have found myself in a similar ditch, asking questions that transcend the moment: What constitutes a truly rich life? How do we leave a lasting legacy? If money isn't enough, what is? And what really matters in the end?

In my quest to answer these questions, I began to ask people, young and old, rich and poor, famous and infamous, what has made their lives rich. Their answers and stories surprised me. And they formed the backstage truths of what you are about to read.

As a young boy in dilapidated jeans, sitting on the edge of the tub, I thought I knew what would make me rich. As a middle-aged man, I'm beginning to discover that truly rich people, whether they know it or not, share six characteristics.

I can't wait to tell you what they are.

PART ONE

Rich People Know the Speed Limit

If given enough time to think it over, most of us know what enriches our lives, what delivers peace, what glues a satisfied grin to our faces. The trouble is, we're driving too fast to notice. We're stampeding toward the cliff. Exhausted and breathless, we Sprint, Quicken, FedEx, Twitter, and text. And the things that make our lives rich are lost in the blur.

The use of amphetamines—known as "speed"—has skyrocketed in the American workplace by 70 percent in the past decade.[1] We take speed so we can get promoted so we can move faster, work harder, and...well, need more speed.

Light is the fastest speed in our universe. The cosmic speedometer clocks out at 670 million miles per hour. The only thing that comes close is the speed of stress.

I once asked an audience if anyone was tired. One gentleman hollered, "I'm too tired to raise my hand." Me too. I'm tired of traffic jams, to-do lists, microwave dinners, and omnipresent cell phones. I'm tired of paying $19.95 for books that tell me how to save money. And I'm tired of trading the things that last for the things that don't—all because of an outrageous obsession with hurry.

But how do we slow down without pulling out of the race?

How do we jump off the roller coaster without getting flattened?

How do we live in a culture addicted to speed?

A few years ago, an unexpected visitor forced me to pull out of the fast lane and look around for the answers.

The richness of our lives is
determined not by the time
we are given—we all have
24 hours a day—but by what
we choose to do with it.

The trouble with being in the rat race is
that even if you win, you're still a rat.

Lily Tomlin

1

Slowing Down in a Sped-Up World

Not far from our home a tiny pond rests, shaded by elder bushes and nourished by underground streams. At night I occasionally stroll past the pond, watching ducks practice their runway approaches amid the choruses of redwing blackbirds and the croaking of mud-drenched frogs. But tonight all is quiet. Tonight a hot, dry summer has taken its toll, and there are no blackbird choruses. No croaking frogs. No splash landings.

The pond is drying up.

Not long ago I felt like that pond. Flat on my back, I was finished. Kaput. Burned-out.

Five years on a treadmill had taken its toll. Five years of chasing dreams but finding little sleep. Of pursuing success but finding little peace. Midnights writing books had been tacked on to 50-hour work-weeks, weekend speaking engagements, and the nurturing of a growing family. Worst of all, the circumstances I will tell you about in chapter 11 had set my life on edge. Each day began at seven and ended about 19 hours later, if insomnia allowed it.

It's the age we live in, I kept convincing myself. It's normal. We rise before our cell phones wake us. We've been watching the time displayed on the ceiling anyway. Shaving and showering, we listen to stock updates, our pulses racing. In the kitchen, breakfast is two granola bars and enough caffeine to power the Starship Enterprise. But the time is not wasted. We are now reading the morning news and updating our blog.

The car starts before we climb in, and the commute is ideal for catching up on the texting we couldn't do while wasting time with sleep. At work we are mainlining the Internet and marveling at the growth of our Inbox. At night we watch a movie on the DVD while checking baseball player stats and e-mails from friends who wonder why we're not returning their text messages about driving their kids to soccer practice.

If there's life on other planets and they have telescopes, I must have looked like I was in a giant pinball game.

I was climbing the ladder with my nose to the grindstone, my shoulder to the wheel, and my eye on the ball. But like a clumsy juggler, I watched helplessly as things began to hit the ground. My life was like the dried-up pond. I listened hopelessly for the blackbird's song, but none came.

I knew, as you do, that we live in a sped-up world. People headed for Europe used to spend months unwinding on ocean liners, breathing deeply of the salt air, savoring novels, and visiting friends. Now we can make the same trip in less than a day, and when we get there, we're itching to be first off the plane. A friend of mine joked that he could tell when his boss was on vacation. "I only get nine e-mails a day from him," he said. "Normally I get ten."

New studies indicate that the amount of time Americans spend working has fallen by almost eight hours per week since 1965, but few would argue that technology now makes it possible to stay connected around the clock.[2] Time-and-motion studies inform us that it takes .014 seconds to open a drawer. I cannot think of one possible benefit to knowing this.

Is the world a better place than it was in the days of the ocean liner? The food may have improved and the restrooms may be more sanitary, but who has time to notice?

Just the other day I was trying to figure out how to operate a newly purchased remote control the size and dimensions of Cuba, and I thought to myself, *Can you believe how much technology is out there that I never asked for?* I mean, who said we need 52 (I counted) buttons on one remote, each of which can perform at least two functions? Who said we need cell phones that work underwater and bacon-flavored floss? Who said we need clocks that make coffee, satellites to find our car keys, and phones that play music? Hey, I love bread makers and microwaves, but what I'd like more than anything right now is to lie down for a full hour without hearing someone's cell phone suddenly start playing the latest pop hit. I've been trying to program my car radio since 1996. I've been squinting at instruction manuals since high school. This is the aspirin age, and my head is pounding. If I had the time, I'd sit down and write a letter:

> Dear Guys Who Come Up with More Stuff:
>
> Please stop. We're fine. We have enough RAM in our computers and enough room in our trunks. Our jets go fast enough now. We can bowl in our living rooms, and we're impressed.[3] You have put nutritional value on our potato chip bags, and we're amazed. But would you put a little thought into an invention that slows us down? That brings families together? That cures diseases? I'm still trying to figure out my e-mail.

But the stuff keeps coming. You can now buy an indoor doggy restroom and a gas-powered blender to use in the backyard. How times have changed since Daniel Boone said, "All you need for happiness is a good gun, a good horse, and a good wife." Experts tell us that each day in America...

- 108,000 people move to a different home and 18,000 to a different state.
- 45,000 new vehicles are purchased.

- 87,000 vehicles are smashed.
- 20,000 people write letters to the president.
- 1.6 billion pounds of food are eaten. (This includes 75 acres of pizza, 53 million hot dogs, and 4.5 million gallons of ice cream and frozen desserts, the most popular being vanilla). Then we jog 17 million miles to burn off all those calories.

Worldwide, we dispatch 50 billion e-mails each day. The figure was 12 billion in 2001.

The increasing speed at which we live is costing us what we should value most. We are crowding each day with more work than it can profitably hold, and it's costing us the undisturbed enjoyment of friends, our health, and peace with God.

Kenneth Greenspan of New York's Presbyterian Hospital claims that 50 percent of all doctor visits are stress-related and that stress contributes to 90 percent of all diseases. Incredibly, anxiety reduction may now be the largest single business in the Western world.

In a recent study of 11,500 ministers, three out of four reported severe stress, causing "anguish, worry, bewilderment, anger, depression, fear, and alienation."

I meet people all the time who feel this way. They feel like I did when I was flat on my back. For them the birds have stopped singing. The pond has dried up. *When will the streams flow again?* they wonder. *How do we find peace in a noisy culture?* they ask.

One night as spring touched down, I took a walk with my daughter, Rachael. Arm-in-arm we followed a cattle path past blossoming violets and dandelions until the ground fell abruptly away to reveal our favorite pond.

Sure enough, the songbirds were back.

Sure enough, the underground streams were flowing once again.

As we tossed small stones into the water, I thought of my own long winter and an airport wake-up call, my catalyst to recovery.

Here's to our town—a place where people spend money they haven't earned to buy things they don't need to impress people they don't like.

LEWIS C. HENRY

2

Speechless in Seattle

He sits in a tiny office, wiping sweat from his brow. For two nights now he has been unable to sleep. Staring at the ceiling. Wondering. Hoping. A smile tugs at the corners of his eyes as he picks up the phone. The place is New Delhi, India. The year is 1958. "I would like to place an order," he says into the receiver. "I would like 10,000 fountain pen caps."

Surprise is registered by silence at the other end of the line. Then, "Just the caps, sir?"

"Just the caps."

"We'll be glad to fill your order, but...well, what do you plan to do with 10,000 fountain pen caps?"

"Here in India," the young entrepreneur explains, "one who has a pen in his shirt pocket is considered both wealthy and intelligent. I will sell only the tops of the pens. It makes no difference if they can write."

Within two days of arriving in New Delhi, every single fountain pen cap has found a pocket. And in this country, where 300 million people live on less than a dollar a day, the entrepreneur has found his niche.[4]

The man with the smile on his face enters his tiny office once again.

The newly purchased ceiling fan has cleared the sweat from his brow. And once again he picks up the phone.

The best stories are those in which we see ourselves, and if we're honest, we won't have to look far in this one. Too many of us spend a lifetime lining our pockets with surface stuff that makes us seem successful, but down below, down where it really counts, we are as empty as a New Delhi pen cap.

Faking It

Nothing has changed. Internet companies now offer a slice of the good life for a fraction of the cost. Can't afford the whole pen? Not to worry. Can't afford the sticker price? No problem. Joy Theatricals in Toronto will have you looking like a million bucks in one of their evening gowns for a paltry $300 rental fee. Highlight it with a "spacious and functional" Suhali leather Louis Vuitton purse for $50 a night (purchase price $4360). Dazzle them with a set of vintage Pucci jewelry for $75 (purchase price $7940).

If you're a guy, you can now be seen in "the coolest toy you can own"—a business plane. No need to cough up millions. Just purchase "fractional ownership" at Pilatus Aircraft by owning one sixteenth of a plane. (The left wing, perhaps?) You'll get 50 hours of flying a year for just $290,000, plus a little something called a $2900 monthly fee for maintenance, pilots, insurance, and hangar costs (and I should mention the additional $1000 for every hour in the air).

But why stop with the plane? United Thoroughbreds is offering racehorses on the cheap. Though yearlings will cost you up to $100,000 and the feeding, lodging, and training could be $35,000 annually, why not horsepool? One share will set you back $1000, and then there's $200 a month for the horse's care, including "rights to come out to the farm and visit the horse."

Are you concerned that friends are unimpressed by the cheap artwork on your walls? With the help of a consultant at the Art Bank, you can choose from 18,000 oil works, sculptures, photographs, and prints from 3000 artists and sculptors. The consult and ensuing installation will set you back a mere $250, and the rental rates vary from $120 to $3800 a year.

And thanks to the Private Collection, you can now fly along the highway in a canary yellow Ferrari F430 Spider, the wind whipping through your hair (or in my case, soothing my sunburned scalp). A mere $31,000 a year will get you 40 to 60 days behind the wheel.

These are ultimate examples of enjoying things without owning them. But most who engage in such expenditures admit that they do so not for the enjoyment they will provide but for the impression they will make.

We have an outrageous obsession with surface stuff, an unwholesome preoccupation with the opinions of others. We're still buying pen caps. Trust me—I'm guilty too.

Rattled Awake

Flat on my back, burned-out and desperate, I began to take an honest look at my life. What was pushing me to travel so fast? To work so hard? I had to admit it was the drive to acquire surface stuff. To give my family the things I never had—a secure future, an exotic vacation, and jeans without patches.

One morning the phone rang. It was the president of a California company asking me to consider a prestigious position in his firm. "We don't know what you make now, but we will triple it," he said.

I had never heard God speak this clearly to me on the phone.

A smile crossed my face. "Wouldn't it be nice to have a little extra money?" I told my wife, Ramona. "You could use a new wardrobe, and I'd love to buy some of the things I've always wanted, like a car that won't quit and a house that won't leak. And the kids will love it too. We'll be close to Disneyland."

My smile was contagious. "I'd love to do some traveling," said Ramona, staring past me out the window. Two weeks later we were on our way to California for a formal interview.

Oak boardrooms and exquisite offices have always intimidated me, but this time I felt right at home. This was where I belonged. My sights were set on a bigger house, a newer car, security, success...all I had to do was squeeze the trigger.

During the interview, I was intrigued by all that the job offered. This was an opportunity to better myself, to work with people, to travel. "How many days a month will I be on the road?" I asked.

There was an uncomfortable silence.

The president looked at me like it was a trick question. Finally he said, "The question isn't how much you'll be gone, Phil, it's how much you'll be home. And it won't be much."

Ramona is normally gentle, but she started kicking my knee under the table. Later that day on the flight home she expressed her concern. "Life is lived in chapters," she said. "Shouldn't this one include three children and a wife who loves you? We'd really like to remember you for more than your rear end going out the front door. Besides, we need to spend more time praying about this."

I thanked her for her opinion, but I wanted that job.

During our layover in Seattle, I renewed my determination to seize the opportunity. As I walked to a nearby restroom, I practiced my acceptance speech. The offer was too good to refuse. I would call California from home. My mind was filled with thoughts of success, of stepping up the ladder, of the stuff I would buy.

Entering a tiny stall, I latched the door behind me.

Suddenly the place began to shake. Lights flickered, doors rattled, and walls shook. For the first time in my life, I was in an earthquake. Now, I don't know if you've thought about where you would like to die, but if you're anything like me, your list does not include an airport washroom.

At last the rattling stopped. The guy in the cubicle next to me drawled, "Did ah do that?"

I was speechless in Seattle.

Brief memories flashed before me: The miraculous birth of our first child. Faces of friends and family. My wife. My kids. But I didn't see one image of an SUV, a yacht, or beachfront property.

Unlatching the door, I fled the room. Grabbing my wife, I thought, *I'll kiss her and let her feel the earth move one more time.*

True Success

Back on the plane, I took out a pen and scribbled these words on an airline napkin:

> I will consider myself a success when I am walking close to Jesus every day. When I am building a strong marriage, loving my kids, and performing meaningful work. I will consider myself a success when I'm making others homesick for heaven.

I'm ashamed to tell you it took an earthquake to alter my definition of what matters most.

Looking back, I can see that my journey on the road to recovery began with a simple statement scrawled on an airline napkin. The statement reminds me that 75 years down this road, no one will talk about what style of house I lived in, what model car I drove, or the thickness of my bank account. Seventy-five years from now, no one will remember how many bestsellers I wrote or how many fountain pen caps lined my pocket.

But the world may be a better place because I slowed down enough to listen to God's voice. Because I learned to be content with the things I did not have.

For in the end, the fridge magnet is right: The things that matter most are not really things after all.

Cartoon of a businessman talking into the phone:
"No, no. Thursday won't work for me.
How about never? Is never good for you?"

3

A Parachute and a Promise

Road signs are designed to steer us safely in the right direction. Some—like the sort police officers point out when it's too late—seem designed only to frustrate us. But occasionally a sign pops up that brings a smile to our faces:

Caution: No Warning Signs Next 21 Miles

Caution: Water on Road During Rain

Emergency 63 Miles Ahead

I once saw a grainy photo of a service station where a sign boldly proclaimed, "Kids with gas eat free." One on the Alaska Highway is my favorite: "Choose your rut carefully. You'll be in it for the next 200 miles."

I know my rut like I know my own pillow. I spent years carving it, addicted to urgency, believing that an ultrabusy lifestyle equaled success. But the rut grew so deep that my engine ground to a halt, leaving me stalled, stuck, and frustrated. An obsession with trying to get ahead had taken me nowhere very fast.

After the earthquake, I tried to get help. I sent out text messages to my Facebook friends hoping they would Twitter someone who could fax or call me. My exhausted body said, "Enough!" And finally I was willing to listen.

First stop was a visit to my doctor. He advised me to take six months off. But how could I? I wasn't a doctor. I had a growing family and a shrinking bank account. Besides, none of us can insulate ourselves from stress. Thousands of years of recorded history have yet to uncover a civilization where life was a breeze.

Over time, three practical truths would begin to seep through to me, easing me from the rut I had traveled in for so long.

1. Laughter is a tranquilizer with no side effects.

Serious students of laughter tell us that the average toddler laughs about 200 times a day. And I think it's true. You whack your head on a tree branch, looking for pinecones with your grandchild, and this is very funny to one of you. But by the time the average toddler becomes an average adult, he registers only 6 laughs a day. Tell me, where did we lose 194 laughs each and every day? I have a theory. I think our sense of humor is slowly sucked from our body when we enter third grade. There our teacher singles us out and sternly requests, "Would you stand and tell us what is so funny?"

By the time we're out of school, we have jobs to think about. We have debts to pay, appointments to keep, and children to diaper. We have homes to finance, cars to fix, and coworkers to confront.

Just before dinner one night, the phone jangled. My daughter, Rachael, who was five at the time, answered: "Now I lay me down to sleep..." Then, clapping her hand over her mouth, she said, "Whoops!"

I'm ashamed to say that as I sat nearby, I was too concerned about who was on the other end of the line to enjoy the hilarity of the moment. After dinner, Jeffrey, our youngest, pounced on me and tickled my belly. I didn't move. He said, "Dad, you don't laugh so good anymore." And it hit me: *Here I am—a humorist—but the laughter is gone.* That night, after tucking in the kids, I pulled out an old Pink Panther movie and began practicing my laugh. Then I determined to spend more time with my kids, studying their laughter to see if it was contagious.

Gloria Gaither says that children laugh so much because they are "so fresh from God." Perhaps she's right. Jeffrey loves few things more than a good laugh. He's a stand-up comedian's dream. He likes to start jokes, but he seldom finishes. Halfway through he is laughing so hard that the punch line is muffled and indecipherable. Perhaps the joke is funnier that way.

We all know that laughter reduces stress, contains no fat grams, and beats the pants off expensive therapy, but how do we develop this sense of humor? First, we stop being so paranoid. We're afraid of grass because of pesticides and dirt because it's dirty and mosquitoes because of West Nile encephalitis. We're afraid of not enough sunscreen because of cancer and too much sunscreen because of vitamin D deficiency. We have bombarded our children with reasons to stay inside, and it's time we shut the news off and sat under a meteor shower. (Whoa, did I snap there for a minute?)

Second, we go looking for the funny in the ordinary. I collect things that make me laugh and sometimes read them at the dinner table. It's surprising how long the children hang around. The latest was a list from a first-grade teacher who gave her students the first part of an old proverb and asked them to fill in the blanks.

> Better to be safe than...punch a fifth grader.
>
> Strike while the...bug is close.
>
> Don't bite the hand that...looks dirty.
>
> Children should be seen and not...spanked.
>
> Where there's smoke there's...pollution.
>
> A penny saved is...not much.
>
> There's no fool like...Uncle Eddie.

In the darkest of times, laughter helps revolutionize our perspective. Like the sun, it can drive away the January blahs and add richness and texture to our lives. Laughter is a shock absorber, a gift, and an instant vacation. It is a smile out of control, a choice, and an art. Comedian Bill Cosby, whose own son was murdered, said, "If you can find humor in anything...you can survive it." I don't think I would have survived my rut without the sacred tranquilizer dart of laughter.

2. There's a heavy penalty for resisting a rest.

A man sent his psychiatrist a postcard: "Am having a great time on vacation. Wish you were here to tell me why."

To my shame, I realized that I had not taken a two-week vacation in ten years. I didn't need a psychiatrist to tell me I was in trouble. Here I was, an author, but I couldn't spell *rest.* In trying to save time, I'd forgotten how to spend it. Where had I learned my work ethic? It certainly wasn't from studying the life of Jesus. Never does the Bible give us any evidence to suggest that he labored in an occupation to the point of constant emotional exhaustion. No one in history accomplished more, yet he did so without acquiring an ulcer. And several times the Bible tells us that he took a break.

In the midst of the darkest chapter of my life, I began to make small but significant changes. The first was to quit arriving at work before everyone else. Then I went cold turkey on the daily newspaper. My paranoia level plummeted. Next was exercising in our local aquatic center and enjoying some hobbies I'd been too busy for. I even painted our shed, and I said no to evening meetings, seldom missing an opportunity to read to the kids.

While painting the shed one Saturday, a battered wooden birdfeeder caught my eye. The years had peeled its paint back, leaving long ugly scars. I spent an hour or two carefully scraping and repainting, filled the feeder with birdseed, hung it near the shed, and watched to see who would take the bait.

Sure enough, an ordinary sparrow descended from the trees, steadied itself on the edge of the feeder and, with me watching, pecked contentedly away at the tiny seeds. Before long it fluttered up into a tree, lowered its head to its chest, and nodded off.

Above, the sky was furrowed with threatening bands of gray, yet the sparrow rocked itself gently to sleep without a care for tomorrow's lodging. Without a thought about its next meal. A tiny sparrow, clinging calmly to a twig, left the rest up to God.

3. There's only one place to find the missing peace.

Bert lived to skydive. When he was a kid he dreamed of it. And during his first year of college, he finally got the chance. He took a lesson, of course. And he listened closely when told what to do: "First, jump when you're told, Bert. Second, count to ten and pull the rip cord. Third, in the unlikely event that the chute fails, pull the second chute open. And fourth, when you get down, a truck will be there to take you back to the airport."

Bert hadn't felt butterflies in his stomach since his first game as starting quarterback. The plane ascended. Bert jumped. After counting to ten, he pulled the ripcord.

Nothing.

He pulled the second cord. It too failed.

"Crud," Bert muttered, "I bet the truck won't even be there when I land."

Though I have yet to skydive, I've felt like Bert. When I was in sixth grade, I lived in terror that my parents would be killed in a car accident. Whenever they left town, I was in torment. The entire time they were gone, I waited for a stern-faced adult to enter my classroom and break the tragic news of the crash. And no one would be there to pick me up after school.

One day while my parents were away, I fled our schoolyard at recess and ran home to throw myself in tears on their bed. Looking up, I saw a tiny picture of a peaceful forest scene. The picture had been placed there before I was born. As a toddler I had taken afternoon naps below that picture. When I was five I had gazed up at it for comfort when my father spanked me. But not until the age of six did I notice that the picture highlighted words written in old King James English:

> Thou wilt keep him in perfect peace, whose mind is stayed on thee: because he trusteth in thee. Trust ye in the LORD forever, for in the LORD JEHOVAH is everlasting strength (Isaiah 26:3-4).

Those were some of the first words I ever read, but I'm just starting to understand them. Every time I strap myself into an airplane, every time I lay awake wondering about tomorrow, I must practice that trust.

The world around us knows little of perfect peace. One authority says that in more than 3500 years of recorded civilization, 8000 peace treaties were broken, and only 286 of those years were spent without war taking place somewhere. What's true for the planet is true for its people. We rarely experience peace. We live anxious lives. We worry. We give in to fear.

Yet tucked away in that forest scene is the key to finding the missing peace we all long for. When an uncertain future looms ahead, God says, *Lift your eyes a little higher.* When unpleasant circumstances close in, God says, *Trust me. I will not let you down.*

Catch Me If You Can

Most self-help books recommend resting the body, but physical rest does not necessarily produce emotional rest. Peace of mind is the direct result of placing our trust in that which will not fail.

My friend Mike Silva takes a message of peace with God to large crowds throughout the world. To illustrate the concept of trust, he once recruited several robust men to stand below the stage and catch him when he fell. As thousands watched, he told the interested onlookers that he was not worried, that he had complete trust in the people below. Then he raised his arms and stepped offstage—backward. Unfortunately, the recruits caught only the bottom half of Mike, and he smacked the ground with a thud. Somehow he managed to crawl back onto the stage, badly shaken, one lens of his glasses shattered. Mike and the crowd learned a valuable lesson: Our trust is only as good as the object we place it in.

One night I took a walk by myself. To my right, a busy highway dotted with road signs stretched on ahead. To my left, sun-drenched wheat fields rolled across the prairies and swelled against the mountains. As cars drove by in a steady stream of traffic, I finally released the things I had held so tightly for so long. "God," I prayed out loud, "I want to trust you completely for my finances, my family, my future... You are big enough to handle them all."

I'd like to inform you that my anxiety vanished for good. But though I lock the door and hide behind the curtains, it visits from time to time. And when I find myself in the same old rut, I need to be reminded that I am loved of God. Period. That no amount of running will impress him. And what I do should be done out of thanksgiving for all that he has done for me.

And I need to be reminded of a parachute and a promise. The parachute tells me that we live in stressful times. But the promise tucked away in a tiny picture is a reminder that we need not worry. God will be there to catch us. Every time.

What is this life if, full of care,
We have no time to stand and stare.

W.H. Davies

4

Fiddler on the Sly

He exits the metro at Washington's L'Enfant Plaza Station and leans a small case against a wall beside a trash basket. Busy passersby take no notice. Though he looks a little like Donny Osmond with a Beatles' style mop top, he's just another middle-aged guy in jeans wearing a Washington Nationals baseball cap. From the case he removes a violin, tosses a few dollars and pocket change into the case as seed money, and starts to play.

It is 7:51 a.m. on a Friday in January. In the next 43 minutes, Joshua will perform six classical pieces for an audience of 1097 people. Each will have a decision to make: *Do I stop and listen or hurry past?*

No one knows that the fiddler is no ordinary guy. Standing incognito against a bare wall, one of the world's finest classical musicians is playing some of the most elegant music ever written on one of the most valuable violins ever crafted. Arranged by *The Washington Post,* his performance is an experiment in speed and beauty and priorities. Will hurried and frantic people pause to listen to soaring masterpieces that have echoed through concert halls and cathedrals for centuries? Or will they hurry on by?

Leonard Slatkin, music director of the National Symphony Orchestra, was asked what he thought would happen. "Let's assume," he answered, "that he is not recognized and just taken for granted as a street musician.

Still, I don't think that if he's really good, he's going to go unnoticed. He'd get a larger audience in Europe...but, okay, out of 1000 people, my guess is there might be 35 or 40 who will recognize the quality for what it is. Maybe 75 to 100 will stop and spend some time listening."

So, a crowd would gather?

"Oh, yes."

And how much will he make?

"About $150."

And who is the fiddler?

Perfect Pitch

The native of Bloomington, Indiana received his first music lessons at the age of four, after his parents found him stringing rubber bands across his dresser drawers and replicating classical tunes by ear, moving drawers in and out to vary the pitch. The rest, as they say, is history. Three days before his rush-hour concert, he had packed Boston's prestigious Symphony Hall, receiving a standing ovation *before* he played. He has soloed with the finest orchestras, appeared on *Sesame Street,* and played the soundtrack on the film *The Red Violin. Interview* magazine said his music "does nothing less than tell human beings why they bother to live." His name is Joshua Bell. And he normally commands $1000 a minute to play.

And the violin?

Handcrafted in 1713 by Antonio Stradivari, the eighteenth-century treasure still boasts the original varnish, which is said to consist of honey, egg whites, and gum arabic from sub-Saharan trees. Twice stolen from its Polish owner, the violin was finally found in 1985 when a New York thief made a deathbed confession. Bell later bought it. The price tag? A reported $3.5 million.

When asked by the *Post* to partake of the metro experiment, Bell insisted on using the instrument and said, "Sounds like fun."

And so it is that he finds himself standing near a shoe-shine stand, short steps from a busy newsstand. Customers line up for lottery tickets.

At their feet are discarded ticket slips from disappointed quick-check customers. Will any of them take note of Bell? One of the likely scenarios the *Post* has considered is what to do if Bell is recognized and word spreads like wildfire. What if people flock to the scene and tempers flare? Would the police be called? Would they need tear gas and rubber bullets?

The performance is captured and later posted on the Internet. The results are painful to watch.

Pearls Before Breakfast

Bell begins with Johann Sebastian Bach's famed "Chaconne," leaning into the music, rising on tiptoe to hit the high notes. Three long minutes pass. Sixty-three people too. Finally one slows enough to turn his head and notice that, my goodness, someone is playing a violin. The act spurs Bell onward. Thirty seconds later, a woman throws a buck into his violin case and hurries off. About six minutes into the performance a solitary fan stands against a wall and listens.

In the 43 minutes that Joshua Bell plays, seven people pause for at least a minute to hear the virtuoso play. Twenty-seven give money. One thousand seventy speed by. Many have cell phones to their ears. Some nurse coffee. Hardly a soul bothers to look.

Calvin Myint passes four feet away. He is listening to his iPod. The song is "Just like Heaven" by The Cure.

J.T. Tillman is impatiently buying lottery tickets. He spends $20 without winning.

Edna Souza is from Brazil. She says later, "If something like this happened in Brazil, everyone would stand around to see. Not here."

The first to stop and watch is John David Mortensen. Like the others, Mortensen is busy. He's a project manager at the Department of Energy with a monthly budget on his mind. But unlike the others, he leans against a wall to listen. Mortensen doesn't know much about the music, but "Whatever it was," he says, "it made me feel at peace." For the first time in his life, he offers a street musician money.

Every single child that walks by tries to stop and watch. And every single time, a parent pulls the child away.

Only one of the 1097 recognizes Bell. Near the end of the performance, Stacy Furukawa can't believe her eyes. She saw the classical star play at the Library of Congress three weeks earlier, and now he is busking for money. She stands ten feet from Bell, a wide grin on her face. "It was the most astonishing thing I've ever seen in Washington," she later said. "Joshua Bell was standing there playing at rush hour, and people were not stopping, and not even looking, and some were flipping quarters at him! Quarters! I wouldn't do that to anybody. I was thinking, *What kind of a city do I live in?*"

When it was over, Furukawa introduced herself to Bell and gave him a twenty.

Future Tense

Now put yourself in the crowd. Be honest. What would you have done? Sadly, I think I would have been with the 1097. I am guilty of being so schedule driven and task oriented that I am unable to find time for divine interruptions. I am convinced that I would have joined the multitude that missed the awe-inspiring music of the moment because they were careening through life, always looking to the future, always saying things like, "When I get to the office, I will..." or "If I can just make it through this week, I can..."

Says Richard Swenson, "Our society is undergoing a gigantic sociological experiment to see exactly how far we can take a ricochet life without imploding."

While in Hong Kong, my wife and I learned a little about pictographs. The Chinese pictograph for busy (*mang*) is composed of two characters: heart (*xin*) and death (*wang*). I asked a wise schoolteacher about this, and he offered this advice: "When your life is too busy, you miss what is most important. When your life is too busy, your heart is dead."

Asking a few questions is helpful—even revolutionary. Has our appreciation for beauty been buried beneath our relentless busyness? When it comes down to those moment by moment choices, what are our priorities? And if we have no time to stop and soak in the sounds of one of the world's greats playing a Stradivarius, what have our lives become?

I almost forgot. You're probably wondering how much Joshua Bell made for his 43-minute performance.

His total take was $32.17.

He later said with a laugh, "That's not so bad, considering. That's 40 bucks an hour. I could make an okay living doing this, and I wouldn't have to pay an agent."[5]

To go faster and faster and do more is to move in the direction of death. Continuous movement, I tell myself, argues a wasted life.

Anne Lamott

5

The Riches of Simplicity

We live in a small town, population 3089 (including pets). You sneeze driving past, and you'll miss us every time. No traffic lights—though there was need of one once. No malls—though my wife has not given up hope. No McDonald's—though someone has started a petition. We've had opportunity to live elsewhere, but this is the suit that fits us best for now.

Some of my best friends are city folk. They love the hustle, the flashing lights, the choices. They thrive on text messages, lunch meetings, and car-pool lanes. Not me. Many weekends you'll find me speaking in the city, but when I point my car homeward, I feel as if someone loosened my tie.

I love living on a street that's so quiet you can sit on your back porch and *listen* to the sunset. I relish waking up each morning knowing that a ten-minute walk to work will knock my cerebral cobwebs loose and that if I leave my car lights on tonight, a neighbor will probably venture out in his slippers and shut them off.

Green Acres

Seems I'm not alone in my craving for the country. In what's been called the "Green Acres" effect, Americans are fleeing cities for the country in record numbers, swapping the concrete jungle for greener pastures. Eighteen of the largest metropolises saw more people move out than move in, according to the latest Census Bureau report.[6] The three largest cities—New York, Los Angeles, and Chicago—lost the most residents. During the most recent four-year span on record, the New York metropolitan area actually saw an exodus of more than 210,000 residents. "Many folks are finding that moving into rural America makes it easier to simplify your life," Wanda Urbanska, author of *Moving to a Small Town,* told *Good Morning America.*[7]

Jim Wiley of Wilmington, Ohio, is one who'd settle for a little more quiet. "Living in Los Angeles, my vision became blurred and twisted," he told *Time.* "I was spoiled. I had secretaries doing everything for me. All I did was talk on the phone and sit in traffic. In L.A. I endured 15 solid years of sunshine. All those rays every day—they aggravated me."

Living in a small town can blur your vision too. You see, it's easier here to slow down to an unhealthy crawl. To sit on the porch each evening watching the bug zapper and forgetting that there's a world out there that could use my help. That's when I need to remember that slowing down in a sped-up world does not mean taking a permanent exit to easy street. God does not call us to rest seven days a week with our head in the sand. He calls us to impact others wherever we are. But in order to do that, we need a quiet place where we can recharge and refocus on the things that matter most. The psalmist wrote, "Be still, and know that I am God" (Psalm 46:10), and Isaiah said, "In quietness and trust is your strength" (Isaiah 30:15).

When my son Stephen was 11, I asked him, "If you had your life to live over again, what would you do differently"?

Before he knew I was kidding, he answered, "Eat more candy."

I laughed at first, but the more I thought about his words, the more I realized the wisdom in them.

You see, I have yet to hear someone in a retirement center say, "I wish I would have spent more time on eBay" or "I wish I would have worried more and laughed less." But I know too many who are spending the last half of a busy life regretting the first half.

Techno Lies

A frenzied friend of mine has this on his desk: "We, the willing, led by the unknowing, are doing the impossible for the ungrateful. We have done so much for so long with so little, we are now qualified to do anything with nothing."

Perhaps a growing number of us are sick and tired of being tired. We're weary of nonstop noise and hurry. We've awakened to the fact that technology promised us more leisure time but it lied. Instead, it doled out ulcers, heartburn, migraines, achy shoulders, and gas. The busyness and noise have been unkind to our marriages, our children, and our fishing, and it's time we said *Enough!* and returned technology for a refund.

One of the sadder letters I received while writing this book went like this:

> When my husband and I were first married, we did not have money for furniture. Our fridge was a cheap icebox that we stocked with ice once a week. We had some memorable water fights, dipping our hands in the icy cold water and chasing each other throughout the house. Laughter filled our home. Ten years ago we struck it rich, but my husband changed. He was constantly stressed, worked longer hours, and soon our marriage evaporated. I would gladly trade all the money in and go back to those days of the icebox.

Claire Owen and Craig Pope won five million pounds in the British lottery on Christmas Eve, five months after their daughter was born. The couple eventually broke up and split the money as well as custody of their child. Said Claire, "We were happier when we were broke."[8]

Lest you think I stand around leaning on my cane and longing for simpler times like the Middle Ages, allow me to quote presidential speechwriter Peggy Noonan, who reminds us that the good old days weren't all that good:

> The life of people on earth is obviously better now that it has ever been—certainly much better than it was 500 years ago, when people beat each other with cats. This may sound silly, but now and then when I read old fairy tales and see an illustration of a hunchbacked hag with no teeth and bumps on her nose who lives by herself in the forest, I think: People looked like that once. They lived like that. There were no doctors, no phones, and people lived in the dark in a hole in a tree. It was terrible. It's much better now. But we are not happier. I believe we are just cleaner, more attractive sad people than we used to be.

Late in life, an anonymous friar in a Nebraska monastery wrote the following words. I can't help grinning as I read them.

> If I had my life to live over again, I'd try to make more mistakes next time.
>
> I would relax, I would limber up, I would be sillier than I have been on this trip.
>
> I know of very few things I would take seriously.
>
> I would take more trips. I would be crazier.
>
> I would climb more mountains, swim more rivers, and watch more sunsets.
>
> I would do more walking and looking.
>
> I would eat more ice cream and less beans.
>
> I would have more actual troubles and fewer imaginary ones.
>
> You see, I'm one of those people who lives life…sensibly hour after hour, day after day. Oh, I've had my moments, and if I had to do it over again, I'd have more of them.

> In fact, I'd try to have nothing else, just moments, one after another, instead of living so many years ahead each day. I've been one of those people who never goes anywhere without a thermometer, a hot-water bottle, a gargle, a raincoat, aspirin, and a parachute.
>
> If I had it to do all over again, I would go places, do things, and travel lighter than I have.
>
> If I had my life to live over, I would start barefooted earlier in the spring and stay that way later in the fall.
>
> I would play hooky more.
>
> I wouldn't make such good grades, except by accident.
>
> I would ride on more merry-go-rounds.
>
> I'd pick more daisies.

Of course, I'm not for playing hooky (believe me, my kids know this), but sometimes I wonder where I got the notion that God is pleased with me only when I'm hard at work. In the same way that I love to watch my children chase one another down a sandy beach and plunge into the water, God is pleased when we go barefoot, when we eat ice cream, when we laugh. In the same way that I cheer when my daughter sinks a basketball (yes, this has happened), so God is pleased when we play.

As a boy, I heard people say they would rather burn out than rust out, and I found myself wondering if there wasn't another alternative. Is life a sprint or a marathon? All these years later, I've noticed that some of those very same people are the most miserable and lonely humans I know. In chasing dreams, they missed waking up to the simple joys around them. In climbing ladders, they failed to see that they were stepping on the fingers of those trying to follow them, and their ladders were leaning against crumbling walls.

I haven't arrived yet. I'm still learning to juggle a busy schedule while enjoying the simple gifts God gives. I'm still learning that there is freedom in slowing down. That there are riches in simplicity. And most of all, I'm learning that there is freedom in following the example of Jesus. After all, he carried the weight of the world on his shoulders but slept soundly in the bottom of a storm-tossed boat. He changed the course of history and still had time to hold little children on his lap.

Will you decide with me to forget keeping up with the Joneses? To stop chasing things we can't cram in our coffins? Whether you find yourself in the car-pool lane or out watching the bug zapper, it can make all the difference.

Normal is getting dressed in clothes that you buy for work and driving through traffic in a car that you are still paying for—in order to get to the job you need to pay for the clothes and the car and the house you leave vacant all day so you can afford to live in it.

Ellen Goodman

6

The Smartie's Guide to Finances

When the financial and housing markets hit the skids, I said to a friend, "This sure came as a huge surprise, huh? I mean it's not like we've been overspending or going into debt in this country. It's not like we would spend money we don't have buying things we don't need to impress people who won't even show up at our funeral. What do you think we are? Crazy people?"

It was sarcasm, like Johnny Carson's remark: "Mail your packages early so the post office can lose them in time for Christmas."

Somewhere around third grade I received my very first allowance. I couldn't believe it. My mother, a Scottish Presbyterian, doling out free money. Had she lost her mind? But I discovered quickly that chores were attached and that if I wanted the money I would have to listen to a brief speech right there in the kitchen. And so I tried to sit still as she offered me all the financial advice I would ever need. If I recall correctly, her little homily sounded something like this.

Say a prayer of thanks whenever you receive money. All that we have is on loan. Be grateful. And stop eating all the cookie dough. You'll get addicted, and it'll ruin your appetite.

Money will serve you well; just make sure you don't serve it.

Always give the first part of it back to God. Ten percent is a great place to start. And smile when you drop it in the offering plate. It's fun to shock people.

Remember that borrowing money is like wetting your bed. You'll feel warm for a while, but it won't last. Hey, quit pulling the dog's ears.

The Tortoise and the Hare is a story about finances. There's no hurry. Don't run after get-rich-quick schemes. Go slow and steady, and you'll be pleasantly surprised at the ending.

If you can't afford the donut, leave it on the shelf. Remember, if your outgo exceeds your income, your upkeep will be your downfall. If you want a ten-cent ice-cream cone and only have a penny, come home and raid the fridge. But not right now. For Pete's sake, back away from the cookies and sit down and listen.

Enjoy things without owning them. We can't afford a motorcycle, but Philip Dawson has one. Here, take him some of these cookies.

Saving money is like dessert. You have to wait for it, but you'll be glad you did. Besides, you may need the money one day to help people who didn't follow these principles. You may go now. Be a good boy.

Other advice would come as I aged, and it would come from those more fiscally astute than my mother. ("Don't pay interest on anything that loses value." "Never cosign a loan." "If you need more money, go out and make some.") But after heeding her simple advice these 47 years, I have discovered that I owe no one anything, that contentment has been my companion, and that during the most recent market crash, I witnessed panic only on television.

John Wesley challenged Methodists to "make all you can, save all you can, give all you can," and I imagine the emphasis may have been on the third part of that exhortation. The early Methodists lived simply. They dressed simply. They founded societies on frugality, not that they might hoard, but that they might give.

In his book *The Decline of Thrift in America,* historian David Tucker traces our cultural shift from saving to spending. He notes that throughout much of American history, we saved up to 15 percent of our income. Then came the 1990s, when credit came easy and borrowing became a way of life. It felt good for a few minutes, but did not last. Today the average American is buried under more debt than at any other time in history.

In fact, the average American now owes more to credit card companies than the average American earned annually in the 1970s.

We had no money for donuts, but who cared? We liked stuff and we liked Christmas. Why not celebrate both all year long? Besides, why worry when you can spend?

And so we converted to the religion of More Is Better. We built houses big enough to hold our stuff but too big to heat. We built cars the size of the Titanic but too big to park.

And we watched our riches bury our treasures.

When at last the financial bubble burst, Americans had one massive hangover. Forty percent admitted being more anxious, 32 percent had trouble sleeping, 20 percent were depressed, and gun sales jumped by 39 percent.

Amid all the fears, many acknowledged returning to the frugal life. They were following Grandpa's advice to "use it up, wear it out, make it do, or do without."

- 40 percent bought more store brands.
- 35 percent clipped more coupons.
- 34 percent held off on doctor's trips because of the cost.
- Bottled water sales went down the drain.
- Sewing machine sales climbed 10.4 percent.
- Health club memberships dropped 27 percent.
- 23 percent haggled more.
- And the average cost of a wedding decreased by 24 percent (to a bargain-basement price of $21,814!).[9]

How bad has it gotten? Some are staying home and getting to know their children rather than going to the movies and eating out. Fathers have been seen throwing baseballs with their kids, leaning over fences talking with neighbors, riding bicycles, and walking their dogs. Others have admitted to reading library books. Fewer people are moving. Houses are decreasing in size. Reservations have skyrocketed at KOA campgrounds. Sales of collapsible marshmallow roasting sticks ($13) are through the roof. Said one campsite manager, "Kids have as much fun here as they do at Disneyland." And the lines for the campground swing sets are shorter than the lines at Disneyland. If this continues, imagine where we'll end up.

It sounds almost sacrilegious to say so, but I'm wondering if all of this isn't more of a blessing than we'd like to admit. The very week I discovered that my retirement savings plan had been devalued by 50 percent and that I would therefore have to work until the age of 112, I sat down and wrote these words:

> Thank you, Lord, for this market crash.
>
> For too long we've chased things that have not kept their promise. For too long we've sacrificed at the altar of stuff, and it's cost us our families and our marriages and our peace. Our false prophets said stuff was the hallmark of your blessing—and we listened. We turned our eyes from the Blesser

to the blessings, from the Giver to the gifts. We confused our wants with our needs and bowed our knee to the god of Mammon. We chased what we did not have, forgetting to be grateful for what you gave us. We have placed our trust in limited resources, when a limitless God offers us the richness of his pleasure and his peace. Forgive us, Lord. Remind us that this life is a short and fevered practice for a game we cannot stay to play. Keep us ever mindful of the eternal, ever aware that we are to store up treasure in heaven, where it won't rust and fade or need insurance, a face-lift, or a makeover. Amen.

The only thing wealth does for some people
is to make them worry about losing it.

Antoine de Rivarol (1753–1801)

7

Stuffing It

I walked into an art store in a mall, and the manager asked me, "Are you a collector?" I know what he meant, but an hour after I stopped browsing, I was still thinking about his question: *Am I a collector?*

We are a nation of collectors, and we are running out of places to put things. We buy, we move, we divorce, we forage through yard sales, and we don't know where to park the accrued junk. Enter the Self Storage Association. It proudly proclaims that Americans stuffed their collective stuff into 51,500 primary storage facilities at a cost of $20 billion last year. The industry grew from about 289 million square feet in 1994 to nearly 2.2 billion square feet by the end of 2007, meaning that by the year 2050, America, Canada, the Black Sea, and much of the former Soviet Union will be covered in trinkets, cookbooks, Cabbage Patch dolls, and other stuff we inherited from Uncle Leo.

According to I Need Storage ("Your Junk, Our Problem"), these are the top five most stored items:

1. old tax returns
2. newspapers
3. collectibles
4. our children's old toys
5. our parents' old belongings

This spike in storage occurred during the most credit-crazed time in history, a time when we went on a plastic-fueled shopping spree and didn't know how to stop. We probably spent more money on nothing than any civilization in recorded history.

The average American home grew from 1400 square feet in 1970 to 2300 square feet today, while the average size of the household shrank from 3.1 to 2.5.

In 1995, Americans borrowed about $11 billion in home-equity loans. By 2008—after countless cable shows convinced us that our homes should be houses of worship with granite countertops for altars—those home equity loans had grown to $1.1 trillion.[10]

Our unending focus on wanting and craving and buying and having has landed us in thick soup. The storage industry is only a manifestation of materialism run amok, but clearly we have stuffed trunkloads of temporary debris into garden sheds, all for the meaningless thrill of knowing that somewhere out there we have it.

We park our cars in our driveways now because our garages are crammed with boxloads of things we once coveted only to find out that it was like drinking salt water to quench our thirst, that having it all didn't add up to what we had hoped, that the thrills weren't cheap, and that we had traded peace for the gnawing sensation that debt was a high price to pay to impress others.

Financial analyst M.P. Dunleavey wrote, "When I drive past those ugly, sprawling storage facilities, or even the bright cheery ones, I feel depressed. Someday these early years of the twenty-first century will be remembered as the Crazy Aughts...and we are not richer, we are not happier, for all that getting and spending."

I have a simple solution. Root through one dresser drawer a day starting tonight. Pick out anything you have not touched in the past year. Place it in a box. Set fire to the box. I'm kidding about the fire, but why not have a yard sale—or better yet, give them away?

Jesus said that if we have two coats, we should put the second one in a storage facility. Or did he? Actually, it was Jesus' cousin John who said, "If you have two shirts, give one to the poor. If you have food, share it with those who are hungry" (Luke 3:11 NLT).

So maybe we could go through our fridges too. But first I think I'll sneak out to the kitchen tonight when my wife is sleeping and start with her cookbook collection.

31 Ways to Simplify Your Life

I'm told the Koala bear sleeps 22 hours a day. I'm not recommending this. But here are 31 ways you can slow your life down a little this month. Why not try at least one a day?

1. Take a child for a walk. Make sure it's your child. (If you don't have a child, borrow one from a friend.)
2. Try everything offered by supermarket food demonstrators.
3. Reread a favorite book.
4. If possible, have a pet.
5. Refrain from envy. Genuinely compliment those who have more than you.
6. Make Sunday a day of rest. Start by leaving your watch off all day. Or at least during the sermon.
7. Learn to say no politely and quickly. Practice on telemarketers if necessary.
8. Learn more about the stars. Then lie on your back and find them.
9. Live by the calendar, not the stopwatch.
10. Each day when you wake up, let your first activity be prayer.
11. Wave at children on school buses.
12. Plan some leisure time each day.
13. Buy a bird feeder and hang it outside your window.
14. Learn to enjoy food. Take longer to eat it.

15. Don't major on minor issues.
16. Attend your child's recitals and plays. Compliment the teacher.
17. Don't give your kids the best of everything. Give them your best.
18. Never miss a chance to read a child a story.
19. When you're alone in the car, sing loudly. Don't forget to roll up the windows.
20. As often as you can, give thanks.
21. Avoid negative or overly competitive people.
22. Wear a wild T-shirt under your fancy suit.
23. Change into casual clothes when you get home from work.
24. When you can, buy secondhand.
25. Remember, God doesn't have a wristwatch.
26. As soon as you can, pay your debts.
27. Find a good reason to laugh in the next three minutes.
28. Forget the Joneses. They aren't so happy.
29. Find something you really like and give it away.
30. Read Matthew 6 and then take a walk and think about it.
31. Observe the speed limit.

No man can tell whether he is rich or poor by turning to his wallet. It is the heart that makes a man rich.

Henry Ward Beecher

8

Lifestyles of the Rich and Not-So-Famous

Some time ago I began asking people on airplanes, online, and in checkout lines one simple question: "What has made your life rich?" One of them turned on me rather abruptly and said, "When people like you leave me alone!"

Thankfully, most found the question a little more interesting, and almost a thousand were good enough to respond. They ranged from bestselling authors to concert pianists to real-estate agents. But regardless of their occupation, most share one thing in common. They are realizing that those who slow down enough to enjoy the simple gifts God gives enrich their lives. Here is a small sampling. I hope you'll enjoy them as much as I have.

"My husband and I were both laid off the week following Christmas. Our despair turned to prayer and then to action. We canceled our cable and cell phones. We sold one car. We shop more carefully now, clipping coupons, sticking to our list, and buying bulk when it makes sense. We used the severance packages to pay down our mortgage, and we cook meals at home now. In March, John found work, but

I'm enjoying the scaled-down, less competitive lifestyle. This summer we will plant a garden for the first time in 20 years, and I have dusted off my sewing machine."

"We picked up an old dog at the pound last year and named him George. His previous owner abused him, and he limps a bit, but when I come home from work, George somehow finds a way to wag about nearly everything. He doesn't seem to care how successful I was at the office or how many sales I made that day. He just cares that I'm home. I grew up with an abusive father, and whenever George greets me at the door, I'm reminded that though we both carry scars from the past, we can do something about our outlook on the future. George's limp reminds me of the need for gentleness in my life. An old dog is teaching me new tricks…and making my life rich."

"One thing that has made my life rich without costing anything is a library card. I've trudged through the sewers of France, gone shrimping off the coast of South Carolina, been in the inner chambers of the White House…all through reading great books. Books have opened a world outside my own. Books have shown me there's more to life than my little existence. Books have broadened my horizons, they have challenged me to take risks, and best of all, they have shown me the true path to God through his Son Jesus."

"I recently rediscovered the Sabbath. Now, instead of shopping, fixing the car, or cleaning the house, our family attends an early church service and then spends the day together. We have hiked into the Rocky Mountains, singing at the top of our lungs like the von Trapp family.

We have serenaded the patrons of old folks' homes. And we have sat under pine trees, reading the classics together. Always we are better prepared for Monday because of Sunday."

"One year ago we left our crowded apartment atop seven flights of narrow stairs in overpriced New York for a bigger fixer-upper house of our own in a small town. Even with our best calculations, we wondered how it would work. I quit my job. My husband took a pay cut. And we were worried. We have spent more on heat, repair bills, and gas to visit family, but our lives are enriched in so many ways. We spend less eating out now, and we have yet to meet the Joneses, though I'm sure they're here somewhere. I just learned that twins are on the way. The same month of their scheduled arrival, our $7000 credit card debt should be erased. Our priorities have changed. Before, we kept promising ourselves that the next month, things would change. They never did—until we changed them. Our investment in a simpler life is paying off. We are resting better and breathing just fine."

"When my husband and I were engaged, the prospect of moving into a house was daunting because all of our possessions wouldn't even fill a room. We had very little money, so purchasing furniture was out of the question. But members of my church gave us a kitchen table with chairs and two big comfortable living room chairs. A landlady gave us a bed and a washer. My mom bought new mattresses for the bed and a couch for the living room. Friends donated shelves, an end table, and kitchen accessories. At four separate bridal showers and the wedding, relatives and friends heaped gifts on us. We have been married now for almost eight years, and when we look around our home, we can recall the names of friends and family who gave certain gifts. If we had been financially well-off, our decor would have been more stylish, but the rooms would not have been filled with the joy of hundreds of friends. Money creates independence, but it can rob us of sharing our needs with others and expressing our joy and thanksgiving at their generosity."

"I am a homemaker with two small children and one husband. In the last year I have learned to look positively on the smallest tasks. When I unload the dishwasher, I think of those who will eat off the forks. When I unload the dryer, I sometimes hug the warm clothes and pray for those who will wear them."

"Money hasn't made my life rich (although I wouldn't mind trying it out for a while), but knowing Jesus has. I am profoundly enriched to know that the Creator of the universe stoops to care about me. He cares when I have a bad day or a bad week or a bad haircut. As the years go by, our budget seems to be shrinking. This month my husband lost his job. Yet God has always taken care of us, and I know that will never change."

"I grew up in Africa. I could tell it was difficult for my parents to make ends meet some months, but we never went without that I can recall. Sure, we never had steak at home, but we had vacations, fishing trips, and bicycles. We even got to see the world. It sounds funny, but to this day if given the choice, I'll take a hamburger over a steak anytime."

"My faith in Jesus Christ has made me rich. I was lucky enough to win a national championship as a pro volleyball player, and my first thought was, *This feeling can't compare to knowing Jesus, being loved unconditionally, having purpose on earth, and being accepted by my Creator.*"

"My father taught me how to fish when I was very young. The fun of catching a big one has never left me, but I'm equally excited to watch my kids or one of their friends reel one in. My dad died this past year, and my son graduated from high school. For his graduation present, we spent a week together fishing in Minnesota. The last night, when we were bringing in the boat, the weather was perfect and the scenery was beautiful. I was pretty emotional, knowing he was on his way to university and this may never happen again. But I also knew that just like me, he would never forget fishing with his dad."

Part Two

Rich People Hit Curveballs

The richest people I know are not those who live easy lives or watch the sun climb into a blue sky every morning. They don't always pick up the phone to good news or live a life without tears and regrets and questions. In fact, their questions are the big ones: "If God loves me, what am I doing in this wheelchair?" "How could my husband have done this to me?" "Does God even care?" "Where do I go from here?" Of the hundreds who responded to my survey on what makes us rich, almost 90 percent mentioned personal triumph over tragedies, like the death of a child, the loss of a home, or the onset of disappointment and heartache. British author Adrian Plass wrote, "I think I have seen more Western Christians fall apart because 'God has let them down' in some practical way than for any other reason."

The stories that follow are about people who have had good reason to fall apart. But they are learning how to stand in the batter's box and swing when life chucks them a curveball. They are learning where to turn when the road takes unexpected turns. They know that those who trust triumph, that those who laugh last, that those who weather the storm do so because their roots reach deep into the soil and hang on to the rock. They have found a God who weeps with us, whose software's default setting is Love, and who gives us enough light for the next faltering step.

The richness of your life is determined not by what life brings you but by what you bring it, not by what happens to you but by how you respond to what happens.

If you don't learn to laugh at trouble, you won't have anything to laugh at when you're old.

Ed Howe

9

While They Were Sleeping

I wish you could meet Jim and Jean Southworth. They're my kind of people. No one understands better than Jim and Jean that when things go wrong, the right attitude is money in the bank.

About 5:30 one morning, the Southworths and their three children were sound asleep inside their sky-blue home on a peaceful street in Salem, Oregon. Outside, a maple tree was flexing its limbs in preparation for a day of providing shade from the summer sun. An array of shrubs shook dew from their branches. Inside, Zack, the eldest Southworth child, awoke, tiptoed to the kitchen, poured himself a drink, and headed back to bed, unaware that on a nearby hillside, things were taking shape that would put a serious dent in his family's day.

On that nearby hillside, the Curly's Dairy delivery truck rolled to a stop for a routine milk delivery. The driver climbed out, whistling a happy tune, and then heard something not so happy. Turning his head, he watched in horror as his vehicle took a turn for the worse. Thanks to a failed emergency brake, it hurtled down the hill backward, gathering speed. The truck jumped a few curbs and took out a startled maple tree. It flattened some unsuspecting shrubs and toppled a picket fence. Finally, it leveled the Southworths' front porch and crashed to a halt in their darkened kitchen.

Zach sat bolt upright, wondering if he'd slammed the fridge door too enthusiastically.

A few years earlier when an earthquake hit, a startled Jim yelled, "A truck hit the house!" This time he sat up in bed, looking a little dazed, and said, "It's an earthquake!"

But it was a truck.

"It was like a bomb went off," recalls Jim, a dentist. He tried to hurry the family out of the house until he heard a panicked voice from outside call, "Are you okay in there?"

"Who is it?" he asked.

"Curly's Dairy," came the response.

When Jean saw the mess, she did what any homemaker would do: She cried over a spilt milk truck. But when she saw the slogan on the van staring out at her from the ruins of her kitchen, the tears vanished. "Here Comes Curly," it said. And Jean started to laugh.

When the dust settled, Jim managed to talk Curly's out of three gallons of ice cream, though he said he would have preferred a year's worth of milk. Jean wasn't so sure she wanted Curly's delivering anything to her house ever again. After all, the front porch was totaled. The breakfast nook was toast. And the front door? Well, no one quite knew where it was.

Home Improvement

Insurance covered the $15,000 damage, and Jim and Jean decided the time was right to do a little renovation. "Our remodeler said we saved on demolition costs," laughs Jean, "although they don't normally use Curly's for that. We're wondering about the poor driver. He's probably in therapy. We hear that Salem customers cower in mock terror at approaching dairy trucks."

With the renovations complete, Jim and Jean decided to throw a party to celebrate the closing of an open house. Guess whom they invited? Curly's. They had handmade signs telling the driver where to park: "Please park in *front* of the house, not *inside* the house. Thanks."

And in the flower beds: "Danger. Runaway truck zone." Through the truck window, guests were served eight flavors of ice cream. And in the kitchen, 67 guests gathered to browse through the accident photos.

"When we first heard the crash and saw the crumpled walls of our house that morning," says Jean, "we thought this was the end for all of us. But once we realized we'd only been smashed into by a delivery truck, we calmed down. Our entryway and kitchen nook were destroyed, but our kids were okay. That's what matters. They thought this was the coolest thing to happen to them since they could remember, and their friends thought so too. Besides, what good would getting upset do?"

Police, reporters, insurance agents, and construction crews gathered, but lawyers were nowhere to be found.

I asked Jean if they ever consider a lawsuit. "Never," she said. "But we were surprised at the number of people who wanted us to. It was fun seeing our story on the front page of the newspaper, but we were left wondering why our reaction was considered so unusual as to be newsworthy at all. That's the way it's supposed to be, isn't it? After all, we're Christians. We're supposed to practice love and forgiveness."

At first, friends who saw the devastation didn't know what to say. But once they found out that the Southworths didn't mind talking about their adventure, they started calling. One told Jean that if she had to get hit by a large vehicle, she hoped it would be an ice cream truck too.

Looking-Glass Lives

For the Southworths, life is a mirror. Frown into it, and it will frown back at you. Laugh with it, and you will find it a kindly companion.

Some may think the Southworths are your garden-variety crazies, and Jim and Jean might agree. But I know from a ten-year friendship that after watching others worry most about the things that matter least, they made a decision to hold things loosely, to quietly commit everything they have to God, and to live their lives with thanksgiving.

"No matter what happens to us, there's always something to be thankful for," says Jean. "In our case, God protected us. The Curly's truck could have easily come into our bedroom instead of the kitchen early that morning. Besides," she laughs, "my husband is a dentist. He's used to filling cavities."

In their annual Christmas letter, Jean wished for everyone "a year of safety, peace, and store-purchased dairy produce."

Nowadays people in Salem call Jean "the ice-cream lady," but she doesn't mind. "Pulitzer prize winners know what the first line will be in their obituaries," she smiles. "At my funeral I'm sure somebody will say something about the day we got creamed by a dairy truck."

My attitude determines whether grief causes a disease in me or a glorious and everlasting reward.

S.I. McMillen

10

How to Live with Empty Pockets

Some writers impress us with Pulitzer prizes and other prestigious awards and plaques of honor. Others earn a far more permanent place in our hearts when their words are taped to our refrigerators. I noticed recently that a friend had fastened these words to her fridge: "Lord, if you can't make me thin, make my friends look fat."

I found myself wondering who wrote the words, and after a little digging, I was finally able to uncover the answer. I think you'll find it as fascinating as I did.

She was nine when her father died, leaving her and her mother flat broke. Their only option for survival was to move to an economically depressed neighborhood to live with the in-laws—a family of ten. Later, she worked as a copy girl at a local newspaper and earned enough money to attend college, where she hoped to pursue her dream of becoming a writer. But as her grades plummeted, the dream fell apart, and a guidance counselor advised her not to consider a career in writing.

Somehow, though, she managed to laugh off the advice and land a job writing obituaries in a local newspaper. Her mother told her that the only thing she accomplished in those days was getting the people to die in alphabetical order. But still she pressed on.

At the age of 20, she was diagnosed with a kidney disorder, which two of her children would later inherit.

Determined to rise above her hardships, she began writing humorous articles about life as a stay-at-home mom. The articles caught on. And before long, she was writing one of the most widely syndicated columns of all time. Fridges and offices worldwide were soon adorned with her quotes. Here are just a few:

- On exercise: "I've exercised with women so thin that buzzards followed them to their cars."
- On friendship: "A friend will tell you she saw your old boyfriend—and he's a priest."
- On husbands: "God created man, but I could do better."
- On housework: "My second favorite household chore is ironing, the first being hitting my head on the top bunk bed until I faint."
- On marriage: "People shop for a bathing suit with more care than they do a husband or wife. The rules are the same. Look for something you'll feel comfortable wearing. Allow for room to grow."

With titles like *The Grass Is Always Greener over the Septic Tank* and *When You Look Like Your Passport Photo, It's Time to Go Home,* her books brightened the lives of millions.

In one column she mused about how God selected the mothers whose kids would have special needs. She imagines him passing a name to an angel and smiling, "Give her a child with diabetes."

The angel would say. "Why this one, God? She's so happy."

"Exactly," smiles God. "Could I give a child with diabetes to a mother who does not know laughter? That would be cruel."

"But, Lord," the confused angel asks, "I don't think she even believes in you."

God smiles again. "No matter. I can fix that. This one is perfect... She does not realize it yet, but she is to be envied. I will permit her to see clearly the things I see...ignorance, cruelty, prejudice...and allow her to rise above them. She will never be alone. I will be at her side every minute of every day of her life because she is doing my work as surely as if she is here by my side."

When asked to write a book about children with cancer, she said no. How could a writer find humor in such a situation? But after talking with children at a special camp for kids battling cancer, she knew she had to. One day she asked one of the children, "What would you want if you had three wishes?"

His words became the title of her book: "I want to grow hair, I want to grow up, I want to go to Boise." The book changed her life.

> Things that were important before don't seem worth worrying about now. I'm more of a one-day-at-a-time person. I think about the three-year-old boy who threw his arms around me and said, "You know what? I'm going to the circus!" The counselor corrected him, saying they were going swimming. Without missing a beat the kid said, "You know what? I'm going swimming!" It didn't matter, he would have gone to the opening of a bottle of aspirin. And it made me think—little things, little moments. Go for them.

In 1991 cancer hit even closer to home when she contracted breast cancer and underwent a mastectomy of her left breast. When she finally got up the courage to show her husband, Bill, the incision, she expected him to be repulsed. "I searched his face carefully for his reaction," she wrote later. "There was nothing there but love."

One year later, in July of 1993, both kidneys shut down, so she started four-times-a-day peritoneal dialysis and, refusing preferential treatment, put her name on a list for a kidney transplant. Of hospitals she wrote, "Getting out of the hospital is a lot like resigning from a book club. You're not out of it until the computer says you're out of it." Of suffering she said, "If you can't make it better, you can laugh at it."

In one column she told of a recurring dream.

She was standing before God, and he said to her, "So empty your pockets. What have you got left of your life? Any dreams that were unfulfilled? Any unused talent that I gave you when you were born that you still have left? Any unsaid compliments or bits of love that you haven't spread around?" And she answered, "I've nothing to return. I spent everything you gave me. I'm as naked as the day I was born."

On April 3, 1996 she was rushed to San Francisco's University of California Medical Center for a kidney transplant. At first it was declared a success. But then complications set in. On the morning of April 22, Erma Bombeck died of heart failure. She was 69.

Every time I visit my friend's house and walk by the fridge, I am reminded of Erma's gentle spunk and wit. And I am reminded that those who turn their back on self-pity and choose joy enrich more than their own life. They enrich the world.

Lord, I pray, *If I can't be wealthy, make me rich in laughter and friends. If I can't be healthy, give me strength for today. If you won't take my troubles away, at least give me joy to face them until the day I stand before you, having spent everything you gave me, with nothing left but a smile.*

With profound potential for good, suffering can also be a destroyer. Suffering can pull families together, uniting them through hardship, or it can rip them apart in selfishness and bitterness.... It all depends. On us. On how we respond.

Joni Eareckson Tada

11

Daddy, Is Momma Gonna Die?

I was writing a humor column on money and marriage when the phone rang. Letting it ring, I finished the sentence. "Someone stole my Visa card, but I haven't reported it yet. The thief is spending less than my wife."

I thought it was pretty funny. The phone call was not. I picked up the receiver: "Hello?" There was silence at first, then words I've never forgotten. Words that made my stomach tighten and my heart pound.

"H-h-help me. Please help, I don't know what's happening—" It was Ramona.

Normally it's a five-minute jog from my office to our house, but I'm sure I was there in two. Bursting through the front door, I found our three young kids on the kitchen floor pouring oatmeal into a stainless steel bowl, crafting their own breakfast. Stephen looked up at me with wide eyes. "Daddy, is Momma gonna die?"

Jeffrey grabbed my hand and wouldn't let go. I tore into the living room, pulling him behind me like he was carry-on luggage. There lay Ramona in a pool of blood, an ugly gash on her leg. Staring at the ceiling above me, she asked, "What day is it? It's Monday, isn't it?"

It was Friday, April 10. The day we embarked on a journey down a road we would not have chosen, one that would change all of us.

Gathering Storm

Until that Friday, life had been a bowl of cherries with few pits. I loved my job as magazine editor. We had a roof over our heads, food in the fridge, and three lively children. Although we'd had them a little too quickly (three in three years), we couldn't have been happier.

I joked with Ramona: "Sure, we have three kids, but we're far more satisfied than the guy who has three million dollars."

"How so?"

"Well, the guy with three million wants more!"

The truth is, we had everything we'd ever dreamed of. A close family. An improving marriage. And to add icing to the cake, my first book had just been accepted by a publisher.

A few months before, however, there were rumblings that a storm was ahead. Waking up in the middle of the night, I would find Ramona pacing the floor.

"What's wrong?" I'd ask.

"I'm fine," she'd reply. "I just can't sleep."

Finally one night she broke down and told me the reason: "I haven't slept in days. I can't stop thinking about the…the disease."

It was Huntington's, a rare neurological disorder that had haunted her since she learned about it in her early teens. On the scale of human misery, the disease ranks high, bringing mental and physical deterioration, nursing homes, and life support systems. "My dad had it, and I have a 50 percent chance of getting it too," she told me when we were dating. "I thought you should know, before we get…um…any further along."

My response was the last thing she expected: "I'd like to marry you someday, Ramona. I love you." After that I barely gave the disease another thought. *We're young,* I convinced myself. *Invincible.*

But by the time our kids were born, three of Ramona's six siblings had been diagnosed with Huntington's, and she knew she was next. The symptoms were there: Lack of sleep, irritability, occasional clumsiness, even a craving for sweets. But at least she wasn't showing one of the other telltale signs: seizures.

On the day of the phone call, she awoke just after I left for work. The last thing she remembers is standing up to pull on her housecoat and then feeling rather dizzy. As she fell, her leg struck the corner of our wooden bed frame.

The Trouble with Love

Quickly I wrapped Ramona's wound and headed for the kitchen. "What happened to Mommy?" I asked Stephen, who was stirring oatmeal while his younger brother added a generous handful of salt and raisins.

"I don't know," he answered. "She was making funny noises, and she didn't talk right. She thinks I'm her dad."

Gathering the three of them into my arms, I held them tightly. "Maybe we should tell Jesus," said Rachael. "Maybe he can do sumpin."

I prayed out loud: "Dear God, help Mommy to be okay. And thank you that you're right here with us all the time."

"Daddy," said Rachael, pulling on my ear, "can we have bweakfast now?"

As the children munched cold cereal, I called my parents, who lived nearby. "Mom," I said, "I'm not sure what's wrong with Ramona. She's not doing too great. Can you take the kids for a while? And… can you pray?" Then I phoned Ramona's mother. Half an hour later she arrived with a warm hug and an optimistic smile. But the smile soon faded.

"You sure it's Friday?" Ramona kept asking her. "I don't think so."

I was standing in the living room, flipping through a phone book for the number of our doctor. Suddenly Ramona's back arched. Her head snapped back. And an agonizing moan escaped her lips. Her face—an ashen grey—tightened, and her body slumped to the floor. I was paralyzed for a second, and then frantically I rolled her over to keep her from choking. "Dial 9-1-1!" I yelled. On the floor, Ramona thrashed her arms and legs, but no breath would come. Grabbing her arms to keep her from hurting herself, I prayed, *Oh God, please, please—*

It was the first seizure I'd ever witnessed. The first of hundreds to come.

The cost of the hour-long ambulance ride to a nearby city was the least of my worries as we weaved in and out of busy traffic. The girl I fell in love with back in high school lay beside me, unconscious. Was this the beginning of Huntington's? Or the end of everything? And what about the children? I traced the veins on the back of her hand and tried to pray. Beside me sat a Christian nurse, a childhood friend, a gift from God. We chatted about all kinds of things, and tears were in her eyes.

"I read an interview with Linda Ronstadt once," I told her. "She said, 'I'll never get married—there's too much potential for pain.' I...I guess I finally understand what she meant."

My friend put her hand on mine. "Ah, yes," she replied, "but you would never have known such joy either."

Tears slid down my cheeks, and I didn't bother wiping them away.

Finding Grace

In the hospital, the endless battery of tests began. CTs, EEGs...you name it, they scanned it. "They scanned my brain and found nothing?" joked Ramona on the morning of the fourth day. I laughed, bent over, and kissed her face. But the outlook wasn't so funny. Doctors, psychologists, and neurologists all had differing opinions.

"This has nothing to do with Huntington's," said one. "I believe she's having pseudo-seizures. She'll get over it."

A veteran psychologist told us that because Ramona had watched her father drown in a flood on the family farm when she was eight, she was probably reliving the trauma. "It's post-traumatic stress disorder," he told me. "Counseling is the answer."

Back home, our family doctor diagnosed her with severe depression and recommended an antidepressant. When I went to pick up the pills, the pharmacist took me aside. "Phil," he said, holding up the pill bottle, "these things were part of the reason my first marriage ended. My wife became a different person when she started taking them. All I can say is, don't let it happen to you. I thought divorce would cure my problems. I was wrong."

During the next few weeks, Ramona seemed to improve. My boss graciously allowed me to carry on my editorial duties at home, and at night after everyone was asleep, I put the finishing touches on my first book, *Honey, I Dunked the Kids.* In a chapter called "Surprise, Surprise," I told the story of our youngest son Jeffrey, born a mere 51 weeks after his sister. "God's grace always accompanies life's surprises," I wrote.

And when the seizures returned with a vengeance, I hung onto those words.

There is a crack, a crack in everything.
That's how the light gets in.

Leonard Cohen

12

I Beg Your Pardon

The following winter, the seizures continued, and the weather didn't cooperate much either. Thanks to a serious breach in climate change, the weatherman delivered unending snowfall and bitterly cold temperatures. After two weeks of it and the prognosis of more to come, we decided to brighten the winter blues with a trip to our town's indoor swimming pool. I pumped the kids up with anticipation of hot tubs and waterslides, only to see them deflated when we discovered that the cold had frozen the engine block in our car and the battery was stone-cold dead. My eldest son was so mad he wanted to set the Ford on fire, something that would have provided us all a degree of satisfaction and some warmth to boot.

I thought of a wise friend's words: "Some wait for the storm to pass, others dance in the rain." Or in our case, the snow.

And so I herded the troops back inside and told them I had something cool in mind, a little something called Plan B. "You sit here and listen," I said, pulling a hat over my nearly frozen head. "See if you can guess what I'm doing."

Grabbing a shovel and propping a ladder against the house, I climbed onto our gently sloping roof. The kids pressed their flat little noses against the kitchen window and watched in awe as their dad caused the heaviest snowfall in history to cascade past our kitchen window. I have seldom felt more powerful.

Before long, I'd shoveled a 6-foot pile of snow into the backyard. And before long, all of us were having the time of our lives jumping off a 12-foot roof into what looked like a giant homemade marshmallow. We hollered. We pelted each other with snowballs. We pretended to be fearless skydivers and Hollywood stuntmen. We even pretended to be warm.

And afterward, sitting around a darkened kitchen and drinking hot chocolate thick with marshmallows, we all agreed: Plan B was way better than Plan A. "I like winter best of all," said Rachael. "We never drink hot chocolate in the summer."

Of course, not everyone feels this way about the cold. The following diary entries tell the story of a couple from Mississippi who move north to sample the marvels of a white Christmas and end up getting a little more than they bargain for.

A Southerner Moves North

> Dear Diary:
>
> *December 8.* It's starting to snow. The first of the season and the first we've seen in years. The wife and I took our hot chocolate and sat by the picture window watching the snowflakes drift down, cling to the trees, and then cover the ground. Ah, it was beautiful!
>
> *December 9.* Awoke to a lovely blanket of crystal white snow covering the landscape. What a fantastic sight! Every tree and shrub covered with a beautiful white mantel. I shoveled snow for the first time in years and loved every minute of it! I did both our driveway and our sidewalk. Later, a city snowplow came along and accidentally covered up our driveway with compacted snow. I didn't mind. The driver smiled and waved. I waved back and shoveled again.

December 10. It snowed an additional five inches last night, and the temperature dropped to around 11 degrees. Several limbs on the trees and shrubs snapped due to the weight of the snow. I shoveled our driveway again. Shortly afterward, the snowplow driver came by and did his trick again.

December 11. Warmed up enough today to create some slush, which soon became ice when the temperature dropped again. Bought snow tires for both cars—almost $800. Fell on my rear in the driveway—$145 for chiropractor. Thankfully, nothing was broken. More snow and ice expected.

December 12. Still cold. Sold the wife's car and bought a four-wheel drive to get her to work. Slid into a guardrail and did considerable damage to the right rear panel. Had another eight inches of the white crud last night. Both vehicles covered in salt and sludge. More shoveling in store. That idiot snowplow came by twice today!

December 13. Two degrees outside. More stupid snow. Not a tree or shrub on our property that hasn't been damaged. Power off most of the night. Tried to keep from freezing to death with candles and a kerosene heater, which tipped over and nearly burned the house down. I managed to put out the flames but suffered second-degree burns on my hands and lost my eyebrows and eyelashes. Car slid on the ice on the way to the emergency room and did more damage.

December 14. Stupid white junk keeps coming down! Have to put on all the clothes we own just to go to the stupid mailbox! If I ever catch the son of a gun who drives the snowplow, I'll chew open his chest and rip out his heart! I think he hides around the corner and waits till I finish shoveling and then comes down the street at 100 miles an hour. Power still off. Toilet frozen. Part of the roof has started to cave in.

> *December 15.* Six more stupid inches of stupid snow and stupid sleet and stupid ice and who knows what other kind of white crud fell last night! I wounded the snowplow idiot with an ice axe, but he got away. Wife left me. Car won't start. I think I'm going snow blind. Can't move my toes. Haven't seen the sun in weeks. More snow predicted. Forget this! I'm moving back to Mississippi.

My Favorite Prayer

To one degree or another, we've all been there, haven't we?

I once read of a mother with a mentally challenged child whom she handled with grace and patience. Every time this little guy ate, he got more food where he wasn't supposed to than where he was. And every time he finished eating, his mother cleaned up the mess without complaining. It was a little bit like a reenactment of the feeding of the 5000. Each day she gave him a small helping, and by the time he was finished she had cleaned up twelve basketfuls of remnants. But during breakfast one hot summer day, things were worse than usual. When she had to duck to avoid getting hit by a syrupy pancake, the usually patient mother came unglued.

After she stopped yelling, her little boy slowly lifted his head, looked at her with big blue eyes, and sang an old country song he'd heard on the radio: "I beg your pardon; I never promised you a rose garden. Along with the sunshine, there's gotta be a little rain sometime."

Her anger vanished, and before long the two of them were laughing.

That precious little guy was telling his mom one of the most profound things either of them would learn and something I was beginning to learn during my long winter: "Hey Ma, life is gonna throw some wild things your way. But keep your head up—it can make all the difference."

So it is with us. In the dead of winter or on a hot summer day, rich people choose well their attitude. The richest people I know don't always understand what is going on. They don't always like what they see. But they have a quiet confidence that God is there in the midst of the mess, and where God is, something good is bound to happen.

It's funny. When you wake up in the middle of the night and reach out to touch your wife in the hopes that she's still breathing, you don't find yourself debating eschatology or Calvinism and Arminianism; you just know you need to hand your cares over to the one who came up with a bazillion designs of snowflake.

One night, after nursing Ramona through another seizure, I propped myself up on a pillow and watched her sleep. My stomach was churning, and a bottle of antidepressants sounded pretty good to me. But instead I reached for the Bible, and what usually happens happened: Words jumped out at me as clearly as if someone yelled them in my ear.

> Rejoice in the Lord always. I will say it again: Rejoice! Let your gentleness be evident to all. The Lord is near. Do not be anxious about anything, but in everything, by prayer and petition, with thanksgiving, present your requests to God. And the peace of God, which transcends all understanding, will guard your hearts and your minds in Christ Jesus (Philippians 4:4-7).

I'll bet the writer had it easy. Actually, no. Paul wrote those words from prison. Disappointed, beaten, and left for dead, he had found a deep and abiding secret.

Paul knew that things were bad all over. He knew that life wasn't fair. He also knew that even though he couldn't control his circumstances, he didn't have to let them control him. And he knew that the one thing he could control was his attitude—he could pray and choose an attitude of joy.

And so I closed the book and prayed my favorite prayer: "God, help." And—oh me of little faith—I wondered if he was really listening at all.

I know God will not give me anything I can't handle.
I just wish He wouldn't trust me so much.

MOTHER TERESA

13

Surprise Endings

On a blustery March day, we received the news. The gene causing Huntington's disease had been discovered at last. And so, one year after the seizures began, we drove to a nearby city for a simple blood test. "We'll be in touch," the nurse promised us. But weeks of waiting turned to months.

Finally I called the Huntington's clinic. "Why so long?" I asked.

"This is a little-known disease," came the honest response. "Public interest is minimal, and there is little funding. We have only a few people working on it, and we've got a tremendous backlog. We're sorry. We're doing our best to keep up."

In July, my book came out and was a hit. Work began on a sequel. I remember sitting in my study doing radio interviews, trying to cheer listeners up. "How can you laugh when life ain't so funny?" one talk-show host asked me.

I talked about our present situation. How our lives could not be described as happy ones, but strangely, some moments were jam-packed with joy. "Joy," I said, "does not depend on sunny circumstances, good news, or happy endings. It comes from knowing that whatever happens, God loves me; that whatever happens, He is preparing a better place for those who love him."

During the ads I would put down the corded phone and sprint to the next room to check on my wife.

In January, the test results were finally in. We could come hear about them on February fourteenth. Valentine's Day.

Come on, I thought, *that's a day for parties, not final verdicts.* Then I realized how fitting it was. On our wedding day, I stood before 300 witnesses and God himself, promising to be Ramona's sweetheart regardless of what came our way. On each Valentine's Day since I had renewed that vow. Besides, I told Ramona one day, "We have to stay together. I've put on so much weight since we were married, I can't get my wedding ring off."

The Party

The night before Valentine's, a group of friends held a party for us. We prayed together, laughed together, and cried a little too. These were the ones who had been there during those ten months. They didn't spout clichés or have all the answers; they had time. Time to listen to music. Time to talk. Time to play Scrabble. And time to play ridiculous games like the one we played that night, where you try to force a rubber band down off your nose using only your cheek muscles.

On February 14, two doctors held the test results in a small envelope. At last one tore it open and looked over her glasses at us: "Ramona, you have the normal gene..." At first I didn't know what she meant. *The normal gene...the normal Huntington's gene? My wife will soon be an invalid?* Then the doctor continued, "...which means you don't have Huntington's." We stood together in disbelief.

"We don't have it?"

"You don't have it."

We repeated our question. They repeated the glorious answer. Hugging the two doctors, we thanked them over and over again. Ramona was clear. The disease could not be passed on to our children.

That night we celebrated the happiest day of our lives with dinner at a seafood restaurant and a movie with friends. Driving home it was as if we had broken through a long dark tunnel. Surely now the seizures would end. But as the months dragged by, the seizures worsened.

"Things will get better," our doctor kept telling us. "It just takes time."

But time was running out. A mere 90 pounds now, Ramona had no appetite and rarely left the house. When she did, some in our small town didn't recognize her. One day as we drove to visit her sister, a seizure laid her flat in the front seat beside me. Terrified, the children cowered in the back seat, crying. I comforted them as best I could, and after our arrival, took them to a nearby McDonald's.

"How are you doing?" I asked.

"Scared," came the reply.

"Me too."

"Is Mommy gonna die?"

"I don't know," I said. "But here's something I do know. God said he'll always be with us. And he's never broken a promise. You can tell him when you're scared. And you can tell me too, okay?"

It wasn't my most eloquent speech, but before long, the kids were laughing and enjoying their cheeseburgers.

Small Miracles

By summer we had seen 21 specialists, scoured libraries for literature, and tried to diagnose the problem ourselves. Well-meaning friends suggested that demonic activity was involved, so we sought wise counsel. We read the Bible's instructions: "Are any of you sick? You should call for the elders of the church to come and pray over you, anointing you with oil in the name of the Lord" (James 5:14 NLT). And so we did. For months Ramona met twice a week with a female counselor. Still the seizures continued.

Every night we lay awake in the darkness, unable to sleep. And sometimes panic overtook me. "What do I do now, Lord? Where do we go from here?" There was only silence. The windows of heaven seemed to be shut, the shutters drawn tight.

Then verses my mother had drummed into me when I was a child came back to comfort us. "God is our refuge and strength, an ever-present help in trouble. Therefore we will not fear, though the earth give way and the mountains fall into the heart of the sea."[1] "'For I know the plans I have for you,' declares the LORD, 'plans to prosper you and not to harm you, plans to give you hope and a future.'"[2]

But even hope seemed to be slipping from our grasp. The seizures worsened, occurring every day and sometimes every half hour. I rarely left Ramona's side, and late one night, after she was finally asleep, I paced our darkened backyard and fell to my knees pounding the ground. "God," I cried, "I can't take it anymore. Please do something."

I would love to tell you that I saw handwriting in the sky or heard an audible voice. But instead, as I stood to my feet, a doctor's name came to mind. We attended the same church, but I'd never thought to ask Dan his opinion. Minutes later I had him on the phone. After listening to my description, he said simply, "I think I can help. Bring her to see me first thing in the morning."

Sure enough. Dan prescribed a simple antiseizure medication all the others had overlooked.

I don't know if I really believed in miracles before that point in my life. But within a week, Ramona was a different person. Her eyes lit up with the sparkle that first attracted me to her. The seizures ended. God had given me my wife back.

Of course, we're not home yet. More tests are ahead. But every day my wife wakes up beside the most thankful guy in the world. I'm thankful that God's grace *does* accompany life's surprises. That in the toughest of times, his grace can help us choose joy over bitterness and help us stay together when our whole world is falling apart.

A world without children is a world without newness, regeneration, color, and vigor.

James Dobson

14

The Angel Jeffrey

When the world-famous septuplets were born, my phone began ringing off the hook. "I guess you're famous," said the first reporter.

"I am?" I replied.

"Not you," he laughed, "your town. It's the birthplace of Bobbi McCaughey, the most famous mother in the world. You know, the mother of the septuplets."

By noon that day, three television crews had arrived. For some reason the town office put them in touch with me, and before long I was fielding questions in the glare of the bright lights. "Do you remember Bobbi very well?" one photojournalist asked.

"As a matter of fact," I told him, "we dated for four years." His eyes lit up. "But we broke up. She wanted too many kids." His eyes were wider than ever, so I informed him that it was a joke, or it might have made the evening news.

The lights dimmed, but the questions persisted. National newspapers and magazines wanted to know if our small town would be naming a street after Bobbi.

"Yes," I said, "It's called Seventh Street."

Were the births a miracle? How could I respond otherwise? After all, I watched our three come into the world one at a time, and it's a wonder their mother lived. If I had to go through this process, I would require so much medication that I wouldn't wake up until the kids were in fourth grade.

That night when we turned on the evening news, there I was. "We had three kids in three years, and I thought *we* had it tough," I said. "Bobbi had seven kids in six minutes. She could use a little help and a lot of prayer."

Whether you had your children one at a time or not, I'm sure you would agree with me that an attitude of thankfulness and a good sense of humor are the keys to keeping your sanity. And hanging signs in each of their rooms: "Checkout time is 18 years."

Tired Tubes

When your children aren't reducing their rooms to rubble and you manage to listen to them long enough, you'll find plenty to laugh about. One kid explained to another, "My mom can't have any more kids because her tubes are tired."

When Jeffrey (our youngest) was only four, I endeavored to remove him single-handedly from a Sunday morning worship service. He was creating quite a stir, judging from the way everyone in the church building was looking at me, so I picked him up and whisked him swiftly toward the back doors of the church. As I did, Jeffrey hollered, "PRAY FOR ME!"

That same year, we invited a prestigious Bible scholar over for supper. Jeffrey seemed to enjoy his company, and when the man asked, "What would you like to be when you grow up?"

Jeffrey put down his fork. "A baseball player, a hockey player, and a football player," he replied. "What would you like to be when you grow up?"

The scholar smiled. "A teacher," he said.

Jeffrey sized him up and said, "But you don't know anything." Thankfully, our friend thought this was the funniest thing he'd heard in a long time.

Jeffrey's older brother, Stephen, was in Sunday school, listening to a teacher talk about Solomon—about his great gift of wisdom and also his great list of wives. The boy thought for a minute, raised his hand, and said, "Wow! He must have had one *big* bed!"

I love the honesty of children. And sometimes, though I hate to admit it, they're far more perceptive than adults.

One night we Callaway boys were sitting on the sofa watching the playoffs. Jeffrey was controlling the remote. When a particularly disgusting ad came on, he squeezed the mute button and said to no one in particular, "I know why they call 'em ads. They keep adding on stuff that isn't true."

The child delights in honesty, which is usually the best policy, but when he was asked to stand in front of our church on Mother's Day and say a few words about his mom, I wondered how he would do.

On Sunday, I sat there in church, regretting that the child hadn't put a little more time and thought into his speech. After all, the rest of the children were older and gave carefully rehearsed eulogies: "My mom is Mother Teresa, Ruth Graham, Suzanna Wesley, all rolled into a trim 110 pounds. And she looks kind of like Sandra Bullock. She can outcook, outclean, outshop, and outwash just about anything on two legs. And I would just like to say that without her, I wouldn't be here to give this speech, which my dad prepared so carefully late last night."

When Jeffrey's turn arrived, I realized he hadn't written a single note down, so I went along to lend some support—maybe do a Larry Kingish interview. Picking up the microphone, I said, "Well, that Mrs. Leo is something, isn't she Jeffrey? How about your mom?"

For the first time in his young life, he was speechless.

"Well…what do you like about Mom?"

"Um…she cooks food for us?" asked Jeffrey as if he wasn't quite sure. "Sometimes?"

This brought no small degree of pleasure to the audience.

"So is she the best mom you've ever had?"

"Yep?"

"Do you have anything else to say about Mom?"

"Nope?"

I was really hoping for more than this. Something like, "Mom, you're the best invention since the remote car starter. When I needed a shoulder, a hug, or a diaper, you had one. When Dad was sleeping, you were awake. You carried me nine months, and you haven't let me down since. I love you, Mom."

Instead he asked, "Nope?" as if it were multiple choice. And we sat down.

The Kissing Bull

Forgive me, Pastor, but I can't remember the message. I'm sure it had something to do with mothers, but I was too busy squeezing my wife's hand and thanking God that she's still alive despite all these blasted seizures. I was thanking God that though her kids have yet to rise publicly to bless her, they often do so in private.

Let me be honest. I was sitting in the pew, battling despair and wondering about the future and worrying about my kids. Has seeing us struggle harmed our children's psyches and jaded them for life? And then I thought of their acts of compassion toward others and of a cold January morning when Jeffrey was only four.

In those days, his first act upon awakening was to make a beeline for the dress-up box at the end of the hall. There he pulled on a Superman cape, a hat, and a belt, got down on all fours, and chased his brother and sister throughout the house. "I'm a kissing bull," he told them. They loved every terrifying minute of it.

But on this particular morning, Jeffrey charged into our bedroom and gave his mom a hug. Then he looked up and noticed there were tears streaming down her face. He couldn't have known that she had just received a shattering phone call telling her that another sibling had Huntington's. He couldn't know that she was wondering if this awful death sentence awaited her too. But he knew enough to pass on the best news he'd ever heard. And so, as only a four-year-old can, he tuned up his vocal cords and sang just a little off key in a tune of his own making:

"I will not be afraid, for God is with me."

This he sang three times. An angel dressed up like a kissing bull. I was so elated about this angelic visit that I almost had to breathe into a paper bag.

Sometimes wacky. Sometimes wonderful. These are the gifts God gives.

You have not lived a perfect day, even though you have earned your money, unless you have done something for someone who will never be able to repay you.

Ruth Smeltzer

15

Deer in the Willow

It's a wonder our willow tree has any life left at all. This spring the deer discovered it. Strolling through our yard from a nearby field, they thought it was a bark buffet. They chewed and ripped and chomped. But nothing seems to kill this stubborn little sapling. Cold winters, nasty winds, ravenous wildlife...somehow it keeps springing back, flexible, resilient, strong. Our Russian Olive is another matter. It thrives in sandy soil; ours is dirt black. It loves a drought; I overwatered it. Last Saturday I spent the entire morning digging its lifeless body from our front yard and laying it to rest in two-foot sections near our backyard fireplace. Then I replaced it with a stubborn little willow.[3]

It's the same with people. Some are Russian Olives. And some are willowlike—resilient, flexible, growing strong. You've met them. People who force you to pause and wonder, *How do they manage to climb out of bed each morning and plant both feet on the floor?* I think of friends whose children battle muscular dystrophy, depression, alcoholism, or drug abuse.

I think of Donna. Her daughter suffered permanent brain damage because of a car crash. Then her husband had an affair and moved out. Then, one awful day just before Christmas, her son Seth and a friend hit a train 500 yards from our house. Christmas Day should not be spent planning a funeral. Oh, and did I mention that Donna battles cancer? She does. Any one of these things would be enough to push me over the edge. I get a hangnail, and I want to flag down cars and tell people about it. So how is it that this modern-day Job can sit across the table from my wife and me, her face beaming, and say, "It's been so hard, but God has been so good. I would never have experienced his comfort and provision, his healing and compassion without walking these roads"?

What keeps her resilient? What helps her spring back?

Chip of Satsuma, Florida, has me asking similar questions. He struggles with early onset Alzheimer's. "I was diagnosed at 49," Chip told me, "or it may have been 50. I can't remember. (That's a joke!) I live with my caregiver wife and sweetheart. She keeps me going, along with the good Lord, of course, who is my best friend. We have been married almost thirty years now. God brought us together long ago and continues to take care of us, despite all that goes along with this. I believe he is in control, and I'm doing my best to enjoy what I can while serving him and others. It keeps me busy sometimes, along with lots of naps because I tire so easily. Laughter is good medicine. I laugh and pass it along to others I meet. The way grows tough, but so many have it worse. I am in good hands, and God says he has plans for me and they are good. I'm just simple enough to believe him."

Here are a few other stories that inspire me, stories about people who are like stepping-stones rising above troubled waters.

Marji Krahn's son Stevie has not spoken a single word in his 37 years. The feisty and determined child learned to walk at six, but there were few other victories. For years, Marji felt utterly alone. She knew beyond a shadow of a doubt that she was inadequate to handle it alone, and so she searched for God. Finally she began to escape to wayside chapels, where she carried on private and sometimes animated conversations with him. She didn't receive an answer to her every question, but what Marji encountered was what all of us want: a compassionate God, big enough to understand her suffering, and as she would soon discover, powerful enough to use it.

Marji would tell you that she was never truly able to offer comfort until she had been comforted by this weeping God. Gradually she began asking that God allow her to help the people she understood best—"those who were fresh out of hope and too worn-out to care." And God answered. Today Marji serves others as a hospice chaplain. She listens and offers a gentle hand on a shoulder, a cup of coffee, or a warm blanket. She speaks a unique language she learned with her son in his world of silence. "God is bringing meaning out of it all by letting me come alongside people and just love them," she writes. "This role suits me well. I'm just there, with my arms open, to pick up the pieces. My whole life has been a training ground for this."

Over and over those who rise above such circumstances tell me this: "Others have it so much worse than I do." Did you catch Chip's words? "So many have it worse." They don't seem to waste much time thinking about those who look as if they have it easy; instead, they have compassion for those who don't.

On Easter Sunday morning, Marji said a final goodbye as Stevie passed into the presence of God. And this is what she told me: "This year Mother's Day was fuller and sweeter and richer than ever before. Perhaps because I now have a son in heaven who is so perfectly whole, and down here I have my other two sons and five grandchildren to love. I am so very blessed."

Don lost his business and his health in the wake of bad decisions made by a trusted business partner and a doctor who was the best man at his wedding. "I haven't figured this thing out yet," he writes, "and each day brings new challenges, but I know that life is too short to spend it mad at others. Or myself. Or God. Besides, I'm so grateful for each new day. I never had time to volunteer before all of this. And God takes care of me."

After being diagnosed with Parkinson's, movie star Michael J. Fox described his development from a person who was "very driven and very ambitious and very consumed by outside things" into a grateful person. "If you were to rush into this room right now," he said, "and announce that you had struck a deal with God in which the ten years since my diagnosis could be magically taken away, traded in for ten more years as the person I was before—I would, without a moment's hesitation, tell you to take a hike...I would never want to go back to that life—a sheltered, narrow existence fueled by fear and made livable by insulation, isolation, and self-indulgence."

Joy grows best in the soil of thanksgiving.

Scott and Connie Mitchell were our neighbors when we were first married. Soon they became our friends. We watched movies together and laughed even if the movie wasn't funny. Connie wanted to know the end of each movie near the beginning, so Scott would lovingly roll his eyes and say, "Watch, you'll see."

By the time the Mitchells entered the ministry at a church in Portland, Oregon, their son Jonathan's behavior had grown dangerous. By thirteen he was abusing alcohol and drugs and soon had graduated to crystal meth. "We dedicated him to God even before he was conceived," says Connie. "He was so loved and wanted. Why was this happening?"

The drugs made Jonathan paranoid, and soon he had purchased a .22-caliber handgun. One awful night he tried to force his way into their locked house to get a pair of shoes. Gripping the gun with his left hand, he shattered the glass, unlocked the door, grabbed his shoes, and left, completely unaware that the weapon had discharged.

Connie came running at the sound and found her husband standing at the bottom of the stairs. The lone bullet had penetrated his pulmonary artery. Scott died in her arms.

Stunned and devastated, Jonathan accepted responsibility and pled guilty. Still, at 23, he was convicted of manslaughter and sentenced to 11 years in prison.

In the weeks that followed, Connie pored over Scott's personal journals. One entry caught her attention: "When I am tested I will come forth as gold."

"I may not know where God is in all this, but I know that he is involved," she said. "I knew that I would drown if I concentrated on the what-ifs, so I asked God to keep me focused on his love and goodness. As that focus became a habit, it gradually became possible to pray that God would somehow bring glory through this mess and use me as his instrument to bring hope to others who are in the midst of pain and grief.

"Scott had told friends that he would gladly give his own life if it would make a difference for Jonathan. And our son has been given a second chance. He finally has a clear mind. He is healthy and drug-free and learning to make wise choices.

"God is helping me see that he has a much bigger eternal plan. He knows the end of the story, and someday we will see the whole picture. In the meantime I am content to trust in his goodness and love."

Connie knows she's not through the valley and that more challenges lie ahead. I'm sure she sometimes wonders how she'll make it and whether God will be big enough—how the movie will end. I like to picture Scott smiling at her courage and her questions and her faith. Perhaps he is saying, "Watch, you'll see."

Part Three

Rich People Are People People

When I asked people what has made life rich, more than 90 percent of the responses used one word: *relationships*. Relationships with friends and spouses, children and grandchildren.

"Friendship is the greatest of worldly goods," C.S. Lewis believed. "If I had to give a piece of advice to a young man about a place to live, I think I should say, 'sacrifice almost everything to live where you can be near your friends.'"

At its best, companionship deepens our joy, lightens our load, and brightens our path. But let's face it, friendships end. Marriages dissolve. People disappoint. Movie star Judy Garland once told a reporter, "If I'm such a legend, then why am I so lonely? Let me tell you, legends are all very well if you've got somebody around who loves you."

Perhaps you feel like Judy. You've carried the burden of failure. You've felt the brush of disappointment. Or perhaps you just long to make a good thing better. Either way, these stories are for you. May they help us realize that the best things in life are closer than we think.

The richness of your life could
depend on one simple question:
If I were to lose everything,
what would I have left?

I'd rather laugh in a tent than cry in a palace.

James Enns

16

Your Own Backyard

In 2008 a 478-carat diamond was unearthed from the Letseng mine in the African nation of Lesotho. Once cut, it was believed that the diamond could sell for tens of millions. It is the twentieth-largest rough diamond ever found.[1] Here is the intriguing story of one of the others.

In the late 1800s, amid the searing heat of an African summer, a farmer stopped plowing his field and stood, wiping his brow and squinting at the horizon. What was he doing here, sweaty and miserable, staring at the south end of a north-bound mule? In the distance, a small band of adventurers—much like the one he had seen a few minutes ago—was heading for the mountains.

If only I could join them, he thought.

Since the discovery of diamonds, thousands of people were dropping everything to join the search for the valuable stones. But not the farmer. He had work to do—fields to till and livestock to feed. Yet the promise of great wealth kept him awake at night and turned his menial tasks to drudgery. One day, when a complete stranger offered to buy his farm, the farmer agreed with a handshake.

At last he was free to pursue his dream.

The search was long and painful. Trekking mile after weary mile across deserts and plains, through jungles and mountain passes, he searched for the elusive diamonds. None could be found. The weeks turned to months, and the months to years. Finally, penniless, sick, and utterly depressed, he took his own life by throwing himself from a bridge into a raging river.

Back home, the man who had purchased the farm carefully tilled the land. One day as he was planting a crop, he came across a strange-looking stone. Carrying it to the farmhouse, he placed it on the mantel.

That very night, a friend noticed the unusual stone over the fireplace and picked it up, turning it over and over in his hands. Finally, he turned to the new owner of the farm and said, "Do you know what you have here? This has to be one of the largest diamonds ever found."

Further investigation proved him right. Before long, similar magnificent stones were discovered across the entire farm, which turned out to be one of the richest, most productive diamond mines in the world.[2]

The times haven't changed much, have they? Just like the man who was so quick to sell the farm, most of us don't take the time to investigate and polish what we already have. In our disappointment with the way things are, in our quest to get ahead, we fail to recognize the wealth in our own backyard. And we end up walking over untold riches every day.

What They Really Need

Recently I met Andrew. A successful insurance and investment consultant, he had spent the previous 20 years of his life "searching for diamonds." But 18 months ago, he made his way back home—only to discover that his house was empty. A note on the kitchen table told him why: "You were never here anyway. Goodbye." His wife of 23 years had taken their teenage son and daughter and moved 1000 miles away, leaving Andrew with a sprawling ranch, two speedboats, and an antique car collection. "I have absolutely everything," he told me. "It's all paid for. But I've never been so empty. I didn't know what I had until it was gone."

Six months ago, suicidal and desperate, Andrew fell to his knees and prayed, asking Jesus Christ to change him, forgive him of the past, and help him face the future. "This may sound crazy," he told me, "but since that day I have experienced more peace than I did during all those years of success. In many ways, my life is the most chaotic it has ever been, but every morning I take my worries and concerns to the living room and spend an hour on my knees trying to leave them with God. Sometimes I find myself picking them up again during the day, but I'm learning to trust him to take care of my family just like he's taking care of me."

Today Andrew is doing all he can to reconcile with his wife and children, but he knows the road ahead is steep. "I thought I was giving them everything they needed," he says. "I guess what they really needed was me."

Andrew talked with me after hearing me speak one night. He said, "Keep telling people about the riches of relationships. I was so busy building an empire, I forgot to build a home. I was so busy working on multimillion-dollar deals that I hardly had time to buy my friends a cup of coffee. I would trade all this stuff in a heartbeat for one good friendship."

I wish I could turn the clock back for Andrew. And sometimes I'd like to turn it back for myself. But like Andrew, I'm learning that relationships, not ranches, make us rich. I'm learning that we make a living by what we get. We make a life by what we give.

But Phil, you may be thinking, *you don't know my family. You don't know my friends. Hey, these people aren't just diamonds in the rough; they're big chunks of coal.*

You may be right, but before you decide, let me tell you about a few crazy friends of mine. Friends I had almost filed into the coal category. But then some unique circumstances changed things for good.

Every man should keep a fair-sized cemetery
in which to bury the faults of his friends.

HENRY WARD BEECHER

17

Two Men and a Lawn Mower

On a muggy night in late August, a new neighbor moved in. His name was Vance, and I thought the world of the guy from the start. We shared the same interests—music, golf, grousing about politics—and he loved to tell me Mennonite jokes until I was physically sick.

"Did you know there is conclusive proof that Adam was a Mennonite?" he asked one day while admiring my Callaway golf club.

"No, I didn't."

"Yeah," he continued, "who else would stand beside a woman who was dressed like that and be tempted by an apple?"

Not only did Vance have a grand sense of humor, he had a gas-powered lawn mower, ripe for the borrowing.

I had a lawn mower myself, but it was electric, and Vance mocked me for it. "Those are for wimps," he said. "You should have a gas-powered lawn mower like mine. A real *man's* lawn mower." I jammed my thumbs in my ears and made raspberry noises with my lips.

One night my lawn mower quit. Gears squealed and sparks flew. It quit so loud, you could hear it quit in Nigeria. And so I prepared a sign and buried it in a yard sale: "Mechanic's dream. Needs work. Use protective eyewear." Then I borrowed the real man's lawn mower and cut our grass in big wide manly swaths.

One week later on a sunny Saturday, I tapped on Vance's door, hoping to borrow it again. No one was home. *We're such good friends now, I'll just borrow it,* I reasoned as I pushed the blue lawn mower back to my yard and began trimming the grass.

The Stump

I'm not sure why I was in such a hurry that day, but when I came to a large stump that protruded two inches from the ground, I thought, *Hey, I could conserve time by going over it rather than around it. After all, this is a gas-powered lawn mower. It will clear The Stump without a problem.*

I was very wrong: *BLAAAMM!* The mower stopped dead, never to start again. Now, I am not a mechanically minded person, but I like looking at things that are broken. I turned it over. Oil was oozing from an open wound. The crankshaft had sustained multiple fractures. I tried the pull-start mechanism. I hurt my arm.

What would you do? When I was just a boy, my father taught me exactly what to do in such a situation. "Sonny," he said, "if ever you borrow something, return it."

So I did. I carefully pushed the lawn mower into the exact spot from which it was stolen—and left on a five-day business trip to Washington DC.

Vance was waiting for me when I returned. In fact, as I pulled into the driveway, he was standing there like a customs official, his arms folded, the intention to hurt me etched on his face.

"Hi, Vance!" I said like a kid caught taking a bite from a block of cheese.

"Do you have a flashlight?" he asked with all the warmth of a rabid wolverine.

I retrieved one from our pantry, thinking to myself, *He's going to club me to death with a flashlight. I didn't wanna die this way.*

Instead Vance took the flashlight and commanded, "Come with me." Obediently I followed him to the backyard and straight over to the crime scene.

It was growing dark, so he flipped the flashlight on and shone it on The Stump. He had poured an entire bottle of ketchup over The Stump. In the grass beside it was the white spray-painted outline of a lawn mower. And a horizontal "Police Line—Do Not Cross" yellow ribbon was tied to the trees.

Vance looked at me with a welcome grin. "We have a suspect," he said.

Then he motioned me over to our garden, where—I kid you not—handlebars protruded from a fresh mound of earth. Taped to a large gray brick was a fitting eulogy:

Here lies Mr. Mower
A life so quickly taken
By a hand so quick to take
He will never mow
What life had
In the grass ahead of him[3]

Expecting Perfection

It's not hard to understand why Vance is one of my very best friends today. If I need some advice, a good laugh, or someone to listen, I call Vance. For one thing, Vance knows how to practice the fine art of forgiveness. He also knows what every good friend knows: If you expect perfection from people, your whole life will be a series of disappointments, grumblings, and complaints. But if you lower your expectations a little and accept people as the imperfect creatures that all of us are, you just may find yourself a lifelong friend.

Vance agrees with the person who wrote this in Proverbs 17:9: "Love prospers when a fault is forgiven, but dwelling on it separates close friends" (NLT).

Our story doesn't end there. After the death of Vance's blue lawn mower, his wife, Sherri, went to a hardware store and entered their name in a drawing for a brand-new red one. And—you guessed it—she won.

Today, all because of me, they have a shiny red lawn mower in their backyard.

I haven't tried borrowing it yet. But I do keep reminding Vance just how lucky he is to have me for a friend.

Life is to be fortified by many friendships. To love and to be loved is the greatest happiness of existence.

Sydney Smith

18

A Tale of Two Friends

Kevin Birch and I grew up together in the same little town. But we seldom bumped into each other outside the ice hockey rink. There was much bumping there—and punching, and hair pulling... and that was in the crowd.

In high school, I took up refereeing. I still don't know why. Maybe I wanted to prepare for parenting, or I needed a few lessons about the depravity of man. One night, while refereeing a game, I watched Kevin (who was not a dentist) attempt to remove the teeth of a fellow sportsman. After stopping the play, I informed him of his crime, and invited him to spend two minutes in the penalty box while thinking of mending his ways.

Skating past me, Kevin let me know that referees were a necessary evil, like the fumes that follow an airplane. He said that I had serious problems with my eyesight and that my nose was crooked. He informed me about people on my family tree I had never heard of and said that I was headed someplace hot and that I was headed there quickly. After reporting the penalty to the timekeeper, I thought of making Kevin sit a while longer, maybe four to six years, but instead I grinned at him.

"So you didn't like my call, huh?"

He shook his head and then surprised me. "Callaway," he said, "I'm sorry. I need to talk. I'll wait for you after the game."[4]

Following the game, Kevin hung his head a little. "It's been quite a week," he said, apologizing again. "Do you have a few minutes to talk?"

The End of Faith

Over a tall glass of Coke in a nearby restaurant, he told me of his struggle with friends, with substance abuse, and with God. I don't know if I said much that night that was helpful. Mostly I used my ears.

"I'm through with this faith in God thing," he said.

"Well, if you ever need a religious fanatic to talk to," I said with a grin, "you know where to find me."

During the next few years, he took me up on that offer with increased regularity. Late at night, the phone would ring, and Kevin would be desperate. "I need you to pray for me. Things aren't going so well."

"I'm not a priest," I'd say, and he would laugh. And while he listened at the other end of the line, I would pray.

The years have passed, and we've both grown up a little. I've watched Kevin come back to God, marry the girl of his dreams, and become a father to three beautiful daughters. I've also watched him become one of my best friends on the planet.

Sometimes when I travel, I ask Kevin to come along. Sitting on a plane bound for Toronto recently, he finally got up enough nerve to ask me an important question he'd been pondering for years: "How did your nose get so crooked?"

"What? It's crooked?"

"Yeah. It looks like it was in a car wreck."

"Well, I broke it twice in hockey, and you remember how skinny I was."

"I've heard you say you needed suspenders to keep your Speedo from falling down."

"It's true. When I was in ninth grade I weighed less than 100 pounds. So I started lifting weights. One day I was bench-pressing 40 pounds, and my arms gave way. Guess where the weights landed?"

Kevin laughed so hard, a flight attendant came to check on us. I thought she would dispense an oxygen mask.

Crunching Peanuts

Twenty-four hours later, while sight-seeing at the CN Tower (the world's largest freestanding structure until 2007), Kevin turned to say something to me and walked nose-first into a huge sliding glass door. He hit it so hard he knocked it off its hinges. The door too. We spent the afternoon in a nearby hospital, where I watched a doctor push, pull, and prod that nose until he was satisfied it wasn't broken. It sounded like a man crunching peanuts.

"If it wasn't broken before," Kevin said on our way out, "it is now."

By the time we headed for home, his nose was twice the size of normal. Black shadows had formed around his eyes. He looked like a raccoon who had taken up boxing. "I feel your pain," I told him. "Good friends do that."

"I wonder where I'd be if you'd thrown me out of the game that night," Kevin said, looking out the window at the pillowy clouds and reflecting on our memorable encounter outside the penalty box. "You probably should have."

"I'm not sure where I would be either," I told him. "And I hope your nose is okay. It looks like it was in a car wreck."

After we got home, a doctor informed Kevin that his nose was broken for sure. In fact, if you saw us standing together, you'd swear we had the same plastic surgeon. Kevin's nose is crooked as a mountain road.

He's a farmer by trade, and when he's out steering a tractor, you'll probably find him praying with his eyes open. "I pray for you," he tells me, "when I remember to. I'm not the best at remembering, but I try. And God reminds me in his humorous way."

Every time Kevin looks in the mirror now, he has a small reminder of me. And every time he hesitates before opening a glass door, he smiles and says a prayer for his friend with the crooked nose.

I am wealthy in my friends.

William Shakespeare

19

Seven Secrets to Great Friendships

Have you seen the virtual pets kids are downloading? Most parents hope it's a passing fad. I checked out the home page of Felix the Cat. Felix has his own *Mewsletter.* When something important happens in Felix's life, subscribers can read about the latest mews. Go to a million other websites, and you can adopt a virtual pet. It will sit on your screen, sleeping or begging for food. By punching the right buttons, you can feed him, walk him, pet him, and doctor him. If you don't, he'll die, and then you can have an online funeral. Next you may want to consider a virtual fish tank. "Be Tank Ful," is the catchy slogan of one. These sites boast all the joys of a real pet but no real responsibility. After all, having a virtual mess is easier than having a real one. I can't help wondering how this will prepare a child for one solitary happening in the real world, but I don't suppose that's the idea.

The truth is, life isn't like that. Relationships are messy. Friendships require maintenance. In fact, friendships are a lot like money. They're easier made than kept.

If you've ever watched a relationship fizzle or had a friend who just drifted away, you've learned this the hard way. All of us, at one time or another, experience difficulties in our friendships. And these days, with the average American family moving to a new home every five years, things aren't getting any easier on the friendship front.

Many people tell me that friendships have made their lives rich. Yet many of those same people wish those friendships were better.

So how can you be a better friend?

When UCLA football coach Pepper Rogers was in the middle of a disastrous season, he lamented to his wife that he had no friends. "My dog was my only friend," he recalls. "I told my wife that a man needs at least two friends, and she bought me another dog."

Perhaps Pepper, along with millions of others, could benefit from the following secrets to great friendships.

1. Accept others. On the way home from church, a four-year-old boy sat in the backseat, singing an old spiritual he had learned somewhere, "It's not my mama or my papa but it's me, O Lord, standing in the need of *praise.*" He had the words a little mixed up, but he nailed the truth right on the head. Very few people would tell you, "You know, I haven't been condemned, belittled, or criticized quite enough lately. Go ahead. Hit me with something awful." Each of us longs to be encouraged, built up, and accepted by others. Good friends know that. Good friends accept people the way they are. They appreciate and praise the uniqueness of others. And they allow their friends the freedom to be themselves.

2. Listen up. After attending hundreds of formal receptions, Franklin D. Roosevelt decided to find out if anybody was really listening to him while he stood in the reception line. And so, one night as admirers shuffled past him with extended hands, he flashed his famous smile and said quietly, "I murdered my grandmother this morning." Guests would automatically respond with comments such as "How lovely!" or "Just continue with your great work, Mr. President."

Not a soul seemed to listen to what he was saying except for one foreign diplomat. When the president said, "I murdered my grandmother this morning," the diplomat leaned close and whispered, "I'm sure she had it coming."

We all are looking for a listening ear. A friend of mine who was voted most popular girl in her entire high school once told me the secret to her popularity: "I listen." From an early age her father had taught her that "everyone on earth is at least just a little bit lonely." I love that advice. An old Spanish proverb says, "Two great talkers will not travel far together." How true.

To ask questions and stick around for the answers is a noble—maybe even angelic—trait. I have done this twice in my life and have found it powerful and magnetic on both occasions. The ability to show genuine interest in others is an admirable quality of a true friend. When people listen to us, we expand and grow.

3. Keep secrets. As a boy, I remember hearing the Jewish folktale of a man who went through a small community slandering the rabbi. One day, feeling suddenly remorseful, he begged the rabbi's forgiveness and offered to undergo any form of penance the rabbi thought suitable. "Go home," the rabbi told him, "find a feather pillow, cut it open, and scatter the feathers to the wind."

Quickly the man did so and returned to the rabbi. "Am I now forgiven?" he asked.

"Almost," came the reply. "Just as soon as you gather all the feathers."

The Bible compares the tongue to an arrow because once an arrow is shot, it's tough to find and bring back. In my experience, nothing destroys more relationships than the arrow of gossip. Many people live by the rule, "If you haven't got anything nice to say about anybody, come sit over here, I'd love to hear about it." But when we gossip, we violate Jesus' commandment: "Do unto others as you would have them do unto you." Proverbs 20:19 says, "A gossip betrays a confidence; so avoid a man who talks too much." Real friends speak well of you behind your back. They are known as people who won't receive gossip, nor will they pass it on. Remember, a closed mouth gathers no foot. Good friends aren't there just to listen to our secrets; they keep them.

4. Sharpen up. Proverbs 27:17 tells us that we are to sharpen each other "as iron sharpens iron."

Years ago a good friend of mine took me out for pie and coffee. "Phil," he said as we ate together, "It's not fun for me to tell you this, but since we talked the other night, I've felt I needed to confront you about something." I set my fork down and listened. "Sometimes you have a real problem with gossip. And it's not helping anyone, least of all you."

I was steamed. Offended. I sat there eating pie, thinking of his problems. How dare he talk to me like this? Who does he think he is? But the more I shut up and ate pie, the more I thought about his words, and the more I thought about them, the more I realized he was right on the money. Today, though we are many miles apart, I consider him to be one of my truest friends.

"Wounds from a friend can be trusted" (Proverbs 27:6) because our best friends stab us in the front. Those who provoke change in us do so because they tell us the painful truth about ourselves. And they mix it with a generous dose of love.

5. Practice forgiveness. When a friend who works in an office near mine came to work one morning, he found a can of Coke on his desk. On the side was a Post-it note bearing these words: "Sorry. I was a jerk. Will you ever forgive me?" Smiling, he walked down the hall with a message of forgiveness. You may have already guessed. The writer of the note was me. And later that day my friend brought me a can of Pepsi.

It is impossible for me to overstate the importance of forgiveness in friendship. We may be the ones who hurt or the ones who did the hurting; either way, good friends humble themselves enough to admit when they are wrong. And good friends forgive. In fact, the gift of forgiveness is often the best gift we can offer a friend. And if it is accompanied by a can of soda, so much the better.

(Of course, it's important to remember that we are not here on earth to please everyone. Some are bound and determined to add us to the growing list of their enemies, so we will have to let them, and we will have to forgive them. Sometimes that means forgiving unaccepting parents who want us to live their dream of having someone in the family become a nuclear physicist. I have a recommendation. Set up an appointment for them with the admissions department at Yale.)

6. Focus upward. An old Turkish proverb goes like this: "He who seeks a faultless friend is friendless." How true. Friends fail. People disappoint. And when we expect too much from our earthly friendships, we damage them. Realizing that the very best friends on earth will disappoint us takes the pressure off our friendships and strengthens them. God does not promise that *people* will never leave us or forsake us. He promises that *he* will never leave. Ironically, those who seek lasting joy only in human relationships end up with a nagging emptiness. The true joy of our lives will come from the most important relationship of all, our relationship with God. In loving him, we learn to love our earthly friends better.

7. Be there. Nothing like sickness or bankruptcy can help us discover who our real friends are. During my wife's illness, her friend Julie informed us that she would be babysitting our three kids each Wednesday afternoon. Ramona had no choice in the matter. And so each Wednesday, Julie would show up and "kidnap" the kids, much to my wife's delight. To this day, Ramona often comments about Julie's kindness. Proverbs 17:17 says, "A friend loves at all times." When possible, be there when a friend needs you. If you can't be there, send a note or make a phone call. (You may want to do that before reading the next chapter.) Perhaps the sweetest thing a friend could say about us is not that we were perfect or that we had all the answers, but that we were there.

Like houseplants, friendships grow slowly over time and require constant watering. Friendships that last a lifetime require nurturing, kindness, and a listening ear. Those who make such an investment find that it pays off all through the years.

Is there someone in your church, on your block, or in your office who needs your friendship? Are you willing to make the effort to reach out to them? I hope so. For we find that life is richer, the horizon is brighter, and the road is shorter when traveled with a few good friends.

One more thing: From time to time, deep thoughts enter my mind, and I spend days kicking myself for not writing them down. This week, two such thoughts came to me and I had a pen along, so here they are. You can quote me if you'd like.

1. My friendships grow in direct proportion to how seldom I say four words: "I told you so."

2. Those blessed with ample friendships either have charm and money or they're good listeners.

3. Beneath the surface of every happy marriage is a husband who can't believe his wife married him. We'll talk a little more about such things when you turn the page.

A man travels the world over in search of what he needs and returns home to find it.

George Moore

20

Life, Love, and Hot Dogs

One Monday morning my wife left me. Packed up some earthly belongings, our only daughter, and a Visa card (this time I'm telling the truth), and headed west for a week, leaving Jeffrey (8), Stephen (11) and me (a little older) to fend for ourselves. For her this was good. She deserved a break. She deserved to surround herself with mountains and hot springs and four of her siblings. But for me? Well…let me say that during those few days I developed a new theory. If you're a theologian you may disagree with me, but here goes:

God invented Eve mainly to help Adam find things.

Adam would be walking around muttering, "Let me see…where did I put those figs?" and none of the animals would tell him. So after God stopped laughing, he thought, *This guy can do without a rib, but not without a wife.* Ever since, men have been pursuing women, largely because we need help finding things. "Honey, do you remember where we parked the silver Winnebago?"

The very day Ramona left, I visited the refrigerator roughly 450 times and found nothing there. Oh sure, there were potatoes, but they weren't mashed. There were noodles but no lasagna. I found a loaf of bread but no sandwiches. These are the things meals are made of.

Stephen ran out of socks on Tuesday, and we were unsure where fresh ones came from. On Wednesday I looked everywhere for my wife's list of meal suggestions. Nothing. Jeffrey couldn't find clean T-shirts, so he wore the same one 24 hours a day. It had a very interesting design. This shirt could tell you what we had eaten the previous five days. Mostly we'd eaten pizza. Sometimes we ordered it in. If we were really hungry we went and got some. For breakfast we ate Fruit Loops, which have all the nutritional value of aluminum hubcaps. For lunch, I phoned friends and told them my wife was gone and then wept openly. No one seemed to care.

I was sure that when the girls came home Sunday, they would find us facedown on the carpet, pale, emaciated, gasping, and surrounded by takeout cartons. "We couldn't find the Rolaids," would be the last words we uttered.

On Thursday we went to a baseball game and consumed our weight in hot dogs. The box told us they contained "actual meat products," which was certainly a comfort. After the final out, Jeffrey rubbed his tummy and let out the cutest little burp. "When's Mom coming home?"

"In six more meals," I told him.

He rolled his eyes and belched again.

I didn't have the stomach to tell the child that although she promised to return Sunday, she was the mother of three young children and had a husband who couldn't find anything, so we may not see her until his high school graduation. I couldn't bring myself to tell him that I was having a recurring nightmare in which Ramona was sitting in the hot springs, swapping childbirth stories with her sisters and saying, "They thought I was coming home Sunday. Ha! I will be home just as soon as chickens lay footballs." And then the mountains would echo with crazed laughter.

On Friday I stopped by the convenience store to snatch up some of the necessities of life: some pop, some chips, and a Rocky video. Standing in line, I felt a tap on the shoulder. It was a classmate from high school. We exchanged handshakes and laughter and a few brief memories.

"How's it going?" he asked.

"Oh, man," I said, laughing, "my wife's gone for a week, so I'm here to pick up some health food. Life's been a little wild lately. How about you?" I asked.

"Well, not so good," he said, looking down and kicking at a floor tile. "My wife's…well, she's been gone on a more permanent basis. She left a year ago, you know…" His voice trailed away as a little girl peeked out from behind him.

"I'm sorry," I said, embarrassed. "I didn't mean to…I'm sorry."

As I write these words, I'm sitting alone at a computer, thinking about life. About love. About grace. I am happy to report to you that Ramona did return.

And that Friday night after I got home from the convenience store, I searched through the freezer looking for ice cream. I found some. And to my surprise I found a whole lot more. Lasagna. Homemade buns. All-beef hot dogs. My wife had put them there for us. I hadn't found the note she left.

I guess that's life.

Sometimes the best things we'll ever have were there all along.

I'd trade my fortune for just one happy marriage.

J. Paul Getty

21

Dr. Phil and Dr. Phil

Since writing books on the topic of family, I often receive letters from readers seeking my wise advice. For instance, here's one from Derek Schuemann of Palm Beach, Florida. He writes, "Dear Mr. Callaway, Who cuts your hair? Woodpeckers?"

Thankfully, Mr. Schuemann wastes little time in moving on to his second paragraph: "I'm getting married this summer, and I could use a little advice. Would you please write something about weddings?"

Now, please understand that I've never considered myself an expert. In fact, I have always made it clear that by the time I have it all together as a husband and a parent, I will either be deceased or unemployed. But that doesn't stop people from writing and phoning and e-mailing me with their questions. It's getting to the point where Dr. Phil could call any day, asking me to come on the show and field questions pertaining to marriage. When this happens, I imagine the scene will unfold something like this…

Dr. Phil (leaning forward on the sofa and grinning at the teleprompter): "Today we want to thank another Dr. Phil for taking time out of his busy schedule to come to LA. His book *The Purpose-Driven Wife* changed my wife's life."

Me (nervously): "Thanks Dr. Phil, it's good to be here. Although… I don't remember writing that book."

Dr. Phil (to audience): "See, I told you he'd be funny. Well, yesterday we met four couples whose marriages were off to rocky starts because their husbands were choosing golden retrievers over children, but today we're here to talk about the Nearlywed Game. Since chocolate didn't cure divorce in Switzerland, and it won't do it here, we need some advice on marriage. I'd like you to meet a young man who is engaged to be married, and Phil will be offering him some expert advice. Will you welcome please Derek Schuemann of Palm Beach, Florida!"

Derek (after sitting on the sofa beside Phil): "Well, first of all, I need to apologize to Phil for a letter I wrote him some time ago. I asked if woodpeckers cut his hair."

Dr. Phil (running his hands over his bald head): "Do they?"

Me: "There's a recession happening on my head, but I'd rather talk about Derek."

Dr. Phil: "You're right. This isn't *The Jerry Springer Show.* Now Derek, you're getting married later this year. What kind of questions do you have?"

Derek: "Well, first off, I'm just wondering how much the wedding will cost me?"

Ladies in the audience: "Boooo…"

Me: "Did you ever wonder why parents cry at weddings, Derek? According to the latest statistics, the average wedding costs a lot more than you will ever make. And that's just the wedding. Marriage and children will follow. It's like hockey superstar Bobby Hull said, 'My wife made me a millionaire. I used to have three million.'"

Men in the audience: "Boooo…"

Derek: "Who should we invite to the wedding?"

Me: "Your closest relatives. Your mother, your father, some brothers and sisters, a rich uncle, a rich aunt…"

Derek: "What about my future mother-in-law?"

Me: "You should invite her too."

Derek: "No, no...What if *she* wants to invite more people?"

Me: "This is very important, Derek. From the start she must respect your ability to take charge. Yes, for too long we guys have sat in the back pew, unwilling to take the upper hand in such matters. For too long we have neglected to make the tough decisions. Derek, whatever you do, LISTEN TO HER."

Derek: "What else should I know before I take the plunge?"

Me: "Realize that your wife will irritate you."

Ladies in the audience: "Boooo..."

Me: "No, hear me out. When we were dating, one of the things I admired most about Ramona was how slowly she moved. I was always in a hurry. She wasn't. I ran through flower beds. She stopped to smell the petunias. I viewed this as a great virtue when I walked her to school in the morning and we didn't arrive until lunch, but now, on Sunday mornings, while I'm waiting in the car resisting the urge to honk, it can DRIVE ME NUTS!"

Dr. Phil (standing in audience now, holding a mike in front of Derek's fiancée): "Phil, it sounds like you could use a little advice yourself."

Me: "We all could, Dr. Phil. We all could."

Derek's fiancée: "Phil, what are the characteristics of a great marriage?"

Me: "A deaf husband and a blind wife."

Ladies in the audience: "Boooo..."

Derek's future wife: "No, seriously, I'm getting married soon too. What can I do to make my marriage last?"

Me: "Leave no alternatives."

Derek: "What do you mean?"

Me: "If you're getting married with anything less than *staying* married in mind, it's the wrong step. Marriage is a lifelong commitment. Regardless of what comes your way, you will stay faithful to your promise. I've been married 27 years, and I can say that few things equal the joy of sitting across the table from my wife and saying, 'Honey, this tomato soup tastes like cardboard, but I love you more every day.'"

DR. PHIL (emotional now, looking into the camera): "I hope you're listening."

ME: "Marry the one you love and then love the one you marry."

DR. PHIL: "Sometimes you make the right decision; sometimes you make the decision right."

DEREK: "Is there more?"

ME: "Yes, much more. Try praising your wife. She'll love you for it once she gets over the initial shock."

DEREK: "I'd really like to have a great marriage. Where's the best place to start?"

ME: "Keep the lines of communication open at all costs. It's the key to a great marriage."

DEREK: "Sorry, could you repeat that? I was thinking of something else."

DR. PHIL: "You'd better listen, Derek. Don't make me put your head in a blender. This ain't my first rodeo, son."

ME: "Marriage will pay great dividends—if you pay interest."

DEREK: "What are some practical ways to make a marriage better?"

ME: "Try harder to keep your wife than you did to get her. Love her. Respect her. Romance her. Be forgiving. Be gentle. Pray together. And use the laundry hamper."

DR. PHIL (looking at the camera): "If you don't agree with that, then somewhere a village is missing their idiot. Phil, tell us about your marriage. Has it been perfect?"

ME: "Well, I have a confession to make. I married the wrong woman—"

ENTIRE AUDIENCE: "Boooo..."

ME: "At least that's what an older man told me a week before Ramona and I walked the aisle. And maybe he was right—she could have done a lot better. Our incompatibilities made for some tough times, but God brought us through them. Imperfect people won't have perfect marriages. But those who walk with God learn to walk together."

Dr. Phil: "Phil, I wish we could go on, but we're out of time. Do you have one more question, Derek?"

Derek: "Yes. I'd like to invite Phil to our wedding. It's on August thirtieth."

Me: "I'd love to come, Derek. But that's woodpecker season where I live, and I'm scheduled for a haircut."

Dr. Phil: "Join us tomorrow, when we'll be discussing Rick Warren's new book, *Making Life Rich Without Any Money.*"

Getting a dog is like getting married. It teaches you to be less self-centered, to accept sudden, surprising outbursts of affection, and not to be upset by a few scratches on your car.

WILL STANTON

22

CDD Confessions

It is Monday night. I've just tucked in the kids, picked up another soft drink, and settled down on the couch. My favorite team is three points behind the Dallas Cowboys. My favorite wife is seated nearby, reading *Women Are from Cleveland, Men Are from the Bronx.*

Suddenly the cordless phone rings.

Picking it up, I listen for a full 15 minutes, saying only, "Uh-huh," and then I hang up, not once taking my eyes off the television set.

"Who was that?" asks Ramona from behind the book.

"Oh, just Biff Slootweg's aunt."

"Well?" she says.

"Well what?"

"Well...we haven't seen Biff since 1976. How is he?"

"Fine," I say.

"Fine? What did his aunt say?"

"She said he's fine."

"Come on. What *else* did she say?" Ramona sets the book aside, a sure sign that I am about to be subjected to relentless district-attorney-type questions that will not let up even after the two-minute warning. So pushing the mute button, I tell her the truth.

The truth is that Biff is fine. Ever since the discovery that his adoptive parents weren't really Iranian spies after all, but were working for Iraq, and Biff started skipping school and began sneaking around the world with them, keeping the CIA informed of their every move. Then came that fateful night aboard the nuclear submarine when they discovered the tiny microchips he had implanted in their earlobes, and Biff was tossed into a Baghdad prison, where he was flogged daily until his dramatic escape in a solar-powered blimp.

"Wow!" says Ramona. "That's amazing."

"See," I say, punching the mute button. "I told you he was fine."

If the previous conversation has the slightest ring of familiarity to it at all, chances are that you too suffer from communication deficit disorder (CDD). Please understand that you are not alone. I, together with millions of others, feel your pain.

After 25 years of a less than blissful marriage, a husband and wife finally agreed to see a counselor. Five minutes into their first session, the counselor turned to the husband and asked, "What would you say has been the biggest problem in your marriage?"

Fidgeting in his chair, the husband replied, "My wife's a lousy communicator. We can't even carry on an intelligent conversation, and I want to divorce her."

"Do you have any grounds?" asked the counselor.

"Oh yes, we do," replied the husband. "In fact, we have 13 acres."

"No, no," said the counselor. "I mean...well, do you have a grudge?"

The husband shook his head. "No, but we do have a carport."

Communication. Most of us understand how important it is, but few of us are adept at it. I must admit that my communication skills leave much to be desired. And they are at their lowest point when my wife stands before me and asks, "Do you think I'm fat?"

The thing about this question is that there is no correct answer. If you say no, it means yes. Yes also means yes. "Sort of" means "absolutely." If you laugh during any of your answers, you could go without a well-balanced meal for weeks.

The Turning Point

During the years since Biff's aunt called, I would like to think I've shown some improvement in the communication area. In fact, here are three things I've learned that, for the most part, have brought harmony, static-free communication lines, and some well-balanced meals into our home.

1. Men and women are different. It's not rocket science, but men and women have different expectations, different aspirations, different needs. For instance, my wife needs nurturing, friendship, protection, romance, faithfulness, and clothes that fit, whereas I need food, sex, and...well, I can't think of anything else offhand. I may be exaggerating, but the point is that we are very different. I have found that when we celebrate our differences, when I put my wife's needs ahead of my own and view my own selfishness more seriously than any faults she may display, we draw closer together.

2. Forgetfulness can be a virtue. One Christmas, after a petty argument, my wife and I did not speak to each other for a full three days. This gave "Silent Night" a whole new meaning for us. The reason for our disagreement was so petty that two days into my vow of silence, I couldn't remember what started it. But when Ramona began sneaking my presents out from under the tree and returning them to fine hardware stores everywhere, the thought hit me: *You know, at one point this wasn't such a big deal.* Then I remembered the words my mother drummed into me when I was a boy: "Be kind and compassionate to one another, forgiving each other, just as in Christ God forgave you" (Ephesians 4:32). *God is in the business of forgiving and forgetting,* I thought. *I'd better be too.*

"Honey," I said, with great difficulty, "I'm sorry. I was wrrrr—" It took some practice, but finally I nailed it: "I was wrong. How can I make it up to you?"

Magic words, these.

As it turned out, she was quick to forgive. She even brought back the presents.

3. Use your ears more than your mouth. Or as Shakespeare put it: "Give every man thine ear, but few thy voice." In our marriages, our friendships, and our relationship with God, we must master the art of listening. I readily admit that I have a long way to go in this area. "Knowing when to say nothing is 50 percent of tact and 90 percent of marriage," wrote Sydney Harris, and the apostle James agreed: "Everyone should be quick to listen, slow to speak and slow to become angry" (James 1:19).

Without exception, the best times with my wife always come along when I listen. When I put her first. When I hit my own mute button and show genuine interest in her world.

Now, I'd better go. The phone's ringing, and it may be Biff's aunt. On second thought, perhaps I'll let my wife answer.

For two people in a marriage to live together day after day is unquestionably the one miracle the Vatican has overlooked.

Bill Cosby

23

Matchmaker, Matchmaker

When things get dull around our house, I like to remind my children that I am arranging their marriages. They usually stop whatever they are doing because they have strong feelings about this. So do my sons' girlfriends. As a young teenager on the verge of dating, I believed that arranged marriages were a horrible idea, like driving through London on the right side of the road. But now that I have kids of my own, I see the benefits.

"In time you will grow to love her," I tell my sons, while thumbing through random pictures I have clipped from my high school yearbook. "A beautiful wife is not for you. But one of these gals will be grateful for your affection. Besides, cat-eye glasses will be all the rage in three or four years."

"Oh, Dad," they sigh. They say those words a lot these days: "Oh, Dad."

When our children were young, my wife and I began watching and praying for suitable mates for them. We even took to carrying pictures of our sons and daughter in my wallet primarily to barter with other parents. Many were eager to participate in dowry negotiations. I once haggled with a couple in Oregon who were willing to sign papers betrothing their two daughters and son to our kids, but when they asked for my house, the talks broke down. (Don't worry, Jim and Jean, I won't mention your names.)

With the average Hollywood marriage lasting approximately 37 seconds, I say we start an organization called Arranged Marriages Work Awesome, Eh? (AMWAE). Our slogan will be "Save money! Your honeymoon can double as your first date!" Here are a few of our credos:

1. The current matchmaking model is broken. Let's tinker with it.
2. You think we don't know and love you? We changed your diapers.
3. Why should marriage be based solely on love and respect when we can get some cattle in the deal?
4. My son thinks tacos are a food group. How could he possibly choose a wife?
5. When our children begin paying rent, we will begin listening to their opinions.
6. You'll always have a story to tell at family reunions.

First Came Marriage

I nominate David Weinlick as president. While a senior in college, David joked to friends that he would be married on June 13. He had a date, a tux, and a ring. The only thing missing was a fiancée. So one week before the big day, he and his buddies launched "The Campaign to Elect Mrs. David Weinlick," attracting worldwide attention and 28 would-be brides to the Mall of America in Minnesota, where friends and family overwhelmingly selected Elizabeth Runze on the second ballot.

The couple's first kiss was at the altar.

Today they have three children and a ten-year marriage. "I guess I'm curious as to why people are so shocked that it lasted," Elizabeth says. Though they went into marriage knowing very little about each other, David feels romantic love is a tad overrated. "Marriage really ought to be more about committing to being together than it is about how you feel at a given moment," he says. "We really work to make life enjoyable."

"First came marriage, then came love" is a tune they've been humming for more than a decade. "I don't think it's that much of a secret," says David. "It's really about how we make it work together. We're committed." A few days after their much-publicized marriage, David told her, "Wow. I don't mean to freak you out, but I think I love you."

I don't mean to freak my children out either, but I think we're onto something here. I won't force them into anything, but I am sold on arranged introductions. And dropping subtle hints. And inviting certain families over. And taking out ads in the newspaper: "Jenny Sanderson. We think you'd make a great wife for our son. Have your parents call us at 1-800..."

Allow me to get serious for about a paragraph. The arranged marriages I've witnessed have turned out pretty well, partly because they were formed and continue to form in community. A friend from Angola told me that upon marriage, couples there are assigned *padrinhos,* a mentoring couple who will be in their lives for as long as the four shall live. I know for a fact that my own marriage would have been a disaster without such people, without the watchful love and care of fellow friends and mentors—some of whom would have punched my lights out if I ditched or failed to cherish and honor the girl I've been learning to love these 27 years.

I'm so excited about this that I'm starting to believe in arranged weddings too.

Think of the money we'll save. I will arrange my daughter's wedding, complete with potluck. A-E bring salad. F-M bring wedding cake. She winces when I tell her this, but she will get used to it. By the way, she's getting married June 13 at the Mall of America.

Please mail all applications to our address here in Alaska, where my children have locked me in a little cabin.

Together we stick; divided we're stuck.

Evon Hedley

24

The Incredible Worth of a Memory

In the Academy Award winning movie *The Killing Fields,* Haing Ngor gave an Oscar-winning performance. Having survived the horrors of the Khmer Rouge in Cambodia, he came to America and was murdered in Los Angeles. At first there was speculation that he had been killed for political reasons linked to the film, but recently the truth came out. When Ngor escaped to Thailand and arrived in America, he had only one possession: a photograph of his precious wife, who was killed while a captive. Ngor had the photo mounted in a gold locket and wore it faithfully about his neck. When a street gang held him at gunpoint, Ngor quickly parted with his $9600 Rolex watch but refused to surrender the gold locket.

"Ultimately," said the prosecuting attorney, "this photo, which meant more to Dr. Ngor than life itself, is the reason why he died."

Most of us, when asked to gauge the richness of our lives, think immediately of people. Those who have cried with us, laughed with us, and shaped who we are. Here are the memories of some homemakers, business people, and authors who have discovered the richness of relationships and wouldn't surrender them for all the world.

"Last week I dropped my BlackBerry and watched it shatter into a zillion pieces. For the next few hours I actually had time to play Ping-Pong with my teenage boys, read an Archie with my preteen daughter, and spend an hour in the kitchen watching and admiring my wife while carrying on a conversation. Imagine that! Every day now I am taking time for family and shutting off the new phone."

"I think I got my crow's-feet as a result of so much time up close and personal with my friends. They know how to help me smile and see the humorous side of life. At the best of times, they seem to understand my past, believe in my future, and accept me just as I am today."

"I travel with a man who just sold one of his smaller companies for $1.7 billion. He has five corporate jets at his disposal and more amenities than I can imagine in a lifetime. During a very frank discussion, I asked him this: 'You've got everything, but what are you missing?'

"He didn't think about it long. 'I wish my boy would get right with God and get right with me,' he said. 'I sold myself and lost my son.'

"I asked the question several months back. Hardly a day has gone by when I have not thought about his answer."

"We have been married 58 years. Even now, when we get in the proper mood, we ask each other, 'Is there anything I could do to make you happier?' Having the freedom to express our desires to each other is vital."

"When a friend moved across the country to a new job, the last thing he did was borrow $50 from me. I told him I would lend it on one condition: that he repay it by sending me five letters with $10 in each. Over the next year, he wrote every few months with updates about his job and his family and his new life. Each of his five letters contained $10. When the last installment arrived, I sent him a letter. It included a check for $50."

"For me there has been no greater joy or satisfaction than serving Christ by serving my family. We are seeing incredible dividends from the investment we have made in raising our kids. As long as we are alive, we'll be celebrating the fact that our three children are deeply in love with Jesus. A Relationship Invested in a Christ-centered Home spells RICH to me."

"The thing that's made my life rich is the same thing that's kept me most without money: my children (we just had number seven). With kids you experience the full range of emotions. Joy, elation, sadness, anger, happiness, sorrow, laughter, tears. You name it, kids will help you experience it. I wouldn't trade a minute with my kids for anything life could have given me without them."

"I am rich because I just had the joy of leading my son-in-law to faith in Christ."

"Recently I became a charter member of a secret society we call the Barnabas Group. It consists of three friends in our office complex who watch for opportunities to encourage other members of our staff. We send attractive little boxes with notes, cards, or a few sticks of gum, and we tell people how much they are appreciated. What a difference this makes around the office. Sometimes we even give ourselves a box so other members of the staff won't get suspicious."

"Shortly after we were married, my husband and I heard about the 24-hour rule. For any purchase over $100, we were to wait 24 hours before purchasing it. In 1990, $100 was a lot of money! Now we still discuss major purchases to prevent buying on impulse."

"I was a 30-year-old atheist on the road to destruction before I met Jesus Christ on Bourbon Street at three in the morning. Never before would I have realized that the greatest wealth would be found outside of my finite existence."

"I am a widowed grandfather who used to think Santa Claus had the right idea: visit people only once a year. But as I near 70 and my health isn't what it used to be, I'm increasingly aware of the importance of the people God puts into our lives. The only time I move quickly anymore is when I pull my grandkids' pictures out of my wallet. They are the best-looking, smartest kids in the world. My children ask me to visit several times a year now. They know what I'll do. I'll visit them, spoil their kids, and go home smiling."

"Many years ago, when my marriage was not so good, I heard someone say that he bought his wife presents and hid them all over the house. I started picking up little things, wrapping them up, and placing them in her dresser, in her makeup case, in the fridge, or with the cleaning supplies. I told a friend this when he was going through hard times in his marriage. He thought it sounded too expensive and would take too much effort. But compared to the financial and emotional cost of the divorce he eventually went through, I would have to disagree."

"This morning I dropped off my fourth and last child at kindergarten. The last 12 years I have stayed home with them. We gave up lots of stuff and potential income, but it was so worth it. I will never regret being there for each child every day. Sure, there were times I thought I was going to lose it, but when I dropped my son off today with tears in my eyes, I thanked God for taking care of us, for all the blessings and all the memories."

"Friends of ours had their home burn to the ground late one night. After carrying their two young children from the house, the father ran back inside and pulled out the most important things he could think of. He ran past the TV set, the DVD, even his wallet, and chose instead their entire collection of photo albums and home videos. His wife keeps telling him what a wise choice he made."

PART FOUR

Rich People Know Where the Buck Stops

Winston Churchill believed that when it comes to money, people can be divided into three categories: "Those who are billed to death, those who are worried to death, and those who are bored to death."

I grew up in the first category. We were so poor that my father put our car in neutral going downhill. At night he unplugged our appliances. One Christmas my brother gave me a hand-me-down toothbrush. With careful use it lasted four years.

But in recent days all that changed. Royalty checks arrived. Speaking engagements multiplied. And we faced new challenges. In childhood I learned that when life doesn't make cents, we can still make it rich. But when we find a silver spoon in our mouths, can we can melt it down and turn it into something useful? How do we live rich with money? What are its benefits? What are its shortcomings?

The apostle Paul lived through both poverty and riches. He said, "I have learned in whatever state I am to be content."

Here are stories of our journey and the value of money—what it can do and what it can't. You are about to meet a cheapskate, a billionaire, and an infamous televangelist. All three are learning a great irony: Those who set their minds and hearts on money are equally disappointed whether they get it or not.

But first, a little quiz to help you smile...

The richness of your life is determined not by what you have, but by what has you.

I made my money the old-fashioned way. I was very nice to a wealthy relative right before he died.

MALCOLM FORBES

25

The Money Quiz

This quiz is scientifically designed to measure your financial savvy, your love of money, and whether or not it will have a chance to ruin you one day. Please circle the answer that most accurately reflects your opinion, keeping in mind that your scores could be tabulated and the results sent to your tenth-grade economics teacher.

1. You are carrying a $5000 balance on your credit card. You plan to...
   A. Pay the minimum requirement on your Visa with your Mastercard.
   B. Put $100 a month on your balance so the debt will be paid in March of 2845 by your great-descendant Biff.
   C. Set your wallet on fire. Your pants if necessary.
   D. You're not imbalanced enough to carry a balance. You pay it off each month.

2. This quote most accurately reflects your view of money:

A. "My problem lies in trying to reconcile my net income with my gross habits" (Errol Flynn).

B. "How much money is enough? Just a little bit more" (J.D. Rockefeller).

C. "I have enough money to last me the rest of my life, unless I buy something" (Jackie Mason).

D. "There's no reason to be the richest man in the cemetery. You can't do any business from there" (Colonel Sanders).

3. Which best describes the way you make purchases?

   A. You overspend only on days that begin with T, like today and tomorrow.

   B. You're happiest when spending, but you worry that you don't have as much stuff as your friends do. You hope you can catch up.

   C. Painfully. Begrudgingly. Only when threatened with live ammunition.

   D. You buy what you need and can afford.

4. When you think about your financial situation, you...

   A. Worry only when it's dark and also during the day. Sometimes you break out in hives.

   B. Give thanks that someone has always been there to lend you more.

   C. Go and count it.

   D. Give thanks that God has never failed you.

5. When you receive your paycheck, you...

   A. Head straight to the bank via the bar.

B. Know that if you just work harder, you can make more next month.

C. Think *save.*

D. Celebrate that you owe no one anything and that you're rich enough to give some away.

6. When planning your annual vacation, you…

A. Like to go where you can overspend.

B. Vacation? You've been too busy to take one since you drove the Ford Falcon to Montana in 1978.

C. Stay only with relatives and arrive only at mealtime.

D. Budget and have a blast.

7. You just received a $100,000 inheritance. You…

A. Blow it big-time on a trip to Spain, Greece, and possibly Mars.

B. Quit your job and watch poker on TV.

C. Bury it behind the woodshed.

D. Spend some, save some, and share some.

8. You're shopping for a house. You…

A. Think big. After all, you'll grow into the payments.

B. Take your cues from those home shows on TV. If they can afford it, so can you.

C. Decide against it—and keep living with Mom.

D. Decide how much house you need and how much you can afford, and you set about making it a home.

9. By the time your child is ready for university, a four-year degree will cost $1.3 million, a farm, two Subway restaurants, and your left leg. Therefore you will…

    A. Encourage your son to run away from home.

    B. Forget school. A college education may add thousands to your son's income, but he'll just spend it sending his own child to college.

    C. Homeschool the kids until they're 38.

    D. Invest what you can in an education fund, teach your child how to earn an honest wage, and trust God for the rest.

10. A trusted friend calls, asking you to help someone in need. You will…

    A. Pretend he reached your answering machine.

    B. Lie about your finances.

    C. Get his name and send a check for $1.

    D. Have compassion.

11. To avoid living off cat food during retirement, you plan to…

    A. Trust the government. They wouldn't let you down.

    B. Start a daily interest savings account when you're 64.

    C. Enjoy nothing today, so you can be happy later. In fact, you're eating cat food now.

    D. Put away what you're able and trust God for the future.

12. You are paying off your mortgage by…
    A. Opting for the 40-year plan. Your children are living in your house now, so they can pay for it one day.
    B. Working 29 hours a day.
    C. Not spending money on anything or anyone else.
    D. Making extra contributions like weekly or bimonthly payments so you can pay it down early.

13. You've just been recruited for your first great-paying job. Tonight you will…
    A. Spend like there's no tomorrow.
    B. Borrow from your parents to buy a smashing new wardrobe to go with your newly financed car.
    C. Consider taking your wife out to Wendy's to celebrate, providing you can find enough cash under the sofa cushions and split an entrée.
    D. Give thanks, create a budget, and arrange to save 15 percent of your salary.

14. Regarding a will…
    A. You thought you only had to say "I will" once in life, so you will trust that your cash, your grandma's cutlery, and your darling Chihuahua with the sweater will be divided evenly among your loving family.
    B. You will have one drawn up the moment you start feeling sick.

C. You will leave a note telling your family that everything is buried behind the woodshed, and may the one with the best lawyer win.

D. You have one. If anything is left when you die, you'd like it to be divided among those you love. These do not include the government but rather your favorite charities and your family. There won't be much though. The last check you write will be to the undertaker. And it may well bounce!

How to score. If you knew that the Ds were the correct answer but found yourself desperately wanting to try some of the others, congratulations! You passed with flying colors. If you circled more than two A's, give yourself an F and read this book four times in the next two weeks. If you found yourself gravitating toward the B responses, please order my book *Who Put My Life on Fast-Forward?* If the C answers appealed to you, thanks for taking this quiz during the Cheapskates Anonymous Convention. Please visit chapter 27 of this book.

The wages of spend is debt.

MARK HEARD

26

Our Money Pit

If you're like most North Americans my age, at some point—usually after about six extra-strength Tylenol and a side order of codeine—you will consider building a house. In my case, the idea hit me back in 1994 when I had a temperature of 103, but it took years before I mustered up the courage to tell my wife. "Honey," I said one evening, "how about we.... um...how about I pour you a cup of hot herbal tea and rub your back?"

She said, "What do you want, Phil?"

I said, "Sweetie, I love you so much, you're like ice cream on my pie. How about we build a house?"

"WHAT?" she exclaimed rather loudly. "We don't have the money."

She had a good point there, so I had to think quickly. "The bank does," I countered.

"You can't rob a bank, Phil. Remember? You are following Jesus now."

Imagine the audacity. "We'll take out a mortgage," I suggested. "Remember the movie *It's a Wonderful Life?* All bankers are like Jimmy Stewart. They exist to help others."

"How much help will we need?" she asked.

"Um," I replied, drawing on the accounting skills I'd acquired back in high school, "I think it will cost quite a bit. But we've been renting now for 15 years, and I figure we've spent $81,000 at it. This way, instead of putting the $81,000 into rent, we can put it into taxes, utilities, interest, and repairs."

She looked at me like she looks at vacuum cleaner salesmen.

"Look," I continued, "it's not like we'll go over budget or anything. We'll just count the cost and then begin. After all, how much trouble can wood, hay, and siding be?"

"But there are thousands of decisions to be made," Ramona reminded me. "We're both the youngest in our families, and psychologists say that youngest kids have difficulty making decisions, don't they?"

"I'm not sure. I don't think so. What do you think?"

"I'm not sure either."

On the morning of June 12, the excavation began. At noon the contractor called on his fuzzy cellular. "We have a slight problem, Phil," he said, which is a bit like the Titanic's navigator warning the captain of ice cubes ahead. "We've hit a pit. A BIG pit."

"Um," I gulped, "why don't you just fill it in?"

"It's not that simple," he hollered. "It's got water in it. Lots of water. You have a spring!"

"How deep is the pit?" I yelled, as his cellular began to fade. "Well," I think I heard him say, "there are Chinese kids swimming in it."

The Mortgage Nightmare

That night, I didn't sleep much for the nightmares. In my dream, our house was an exact replica of the Titanic. As we sat around the dining room table, calmly eating our exotic dinner, the ship began tilting to starboard. Fine china plates slid across the table, and water began pouring in the windows. Leonardo DeCaprio fell off the bow. Outside, neighbors rowed by with no room in their lifeboats, holding their hands over their hearts. The last sound they heard as we sank slowly out of sight was Celine Dion's eerie lullaby: "My Mortgage Will Go On."

I awoke in a cold sweat. "A man's home is his hassle," I said out loud. Ramona stirred beside me. "Chicken soup," she said incoherently, and then she awoke and asked me what was wrong. "The pit," I said. "Do you have any idea how much it will cost to build a solid foundation now?"

"We could sell bottled water," she offered. "Callaway Springs. We'll start a rumor about seeing the Pope's reflection in it. People will come from everywhere."

"The water's green," I said. "It tastes like weed killer."

She patted my chest. "It's just money, honey. We can do without some things. Furniture. Windows. Heat." Then she reminded me of a sermon I'd just preached. A sermon on trust. "You think God doesn't know about this?" she asked. "It'll be fine." Then we prayed together, and I rolled over and slept like a baby—waking up and screaming every few minutes.

After five months and six ulcers, we had become a SITCOM family: Single Income Three Children Oppressive Mortgage. We also had a different address. And a new view. Sometimes I found myself saying things I never thought I'd say. Things like, "Hey! You kids clean that lipstick off the wall RIGHT NOW!" or "Jeffrey, if I catch you pounding nails into that oak door again I'll call the police!"

"It's just a house," my wife reminded me three times an hour. Thankfully, the house had the most solid foundation in town. An engineer spent a good hour sampling our soil for proof. "It's unsinkable," he smiled, dropping a $600 invoice into my hands. Hmmm...where had I heard those words before?

One night I went to bed exhausted, only to have our daughter, Rachael crawl in beside me. "Daddy," she said, folding her hands behind her head and gazing at the freshly painted ceiling, "I like the old house better."

"Why?" I asked sleepily.

"I just like it," she said. "You don't read to us here. You've been sorta cranky." And I was wide awake.

We had a family powwow then. We talked of taking care of the stuff God gives us. About giving it all back to him. And I said words I'm learning to formulate: "I'm sorry." Then we prayed together. "Dear God," I said, "I've been so busy building a house that I've forgotten to build a home. Please forgive me." My wife thanked God for new things. For new houses. For new starts. After reading to the kids, I went to bed and slept like a baby—without the screaming.

A friend asked me what one feature in our new house I enjoy more than any other. I thought for a minute and then told him about my bathtub. I spent an extra $175 on a tub that is larger than normal and has jets that shoot water at you. You can toss in a grape and watch it turn into a raisin.

Sometimes at night I enjoyed relaxing in the tub and reading a favorite book. Occasionally I caught myself dreaming of what I would do differently if I were crazy enough to build again, but then I realized how silly that is and started thanking God for what He had given me. For a house that was still afloat. A family that was still intact. And a tub that was just my size.

Often as I relaxed in the tub, I sat there thinking, *If only I had enough money to put water in it.*

Misers aren't much fun to live with, but they make wonderful ancestors.

TERRY GLASPEY

27

The Trouble with Cheapskates

For as long as I can remember, I have been a cheapskate. Just ask Willie Major, a former friend of mine. When Willie was five and I was old enough to know better, we borrowed his mother's change purse while she wasn't looking and set off in search of a candy store. Knowing that I was older and wiser and could be trusted completely, Willie put me in charge of the purse strings. On the way to the store, I untied those purse strings and offered Willy some free advice:

"The copper ones are best," I informed him as the pennies slid slowly between my fingers. "You really wanna hold onto these babies. But see these silver ones? These are no good. You give these to someone else. Someone like me." (Willie has now changed his name to Will and become a lawyer.)[1]

Forty years have passed, and I trust my ethics have improved. But I must admit, I'm still as cheap as a yard-sale eight-track.

When our children were about three and a half feet, my book publisher offered us the use of a condo overlooking the Pacific. So we piled the kids into our rusting Ford and drove down the coast of Oregon. It was a cheapskate's dream vacation: free maid service, free parking, even a McDonald's nearby where you could get a Big Mac on a layaway plan.

Now you must understand that although I'm cheap, I have a deep appreciation of the luxuries others have paid for. In fact, my idea of roughing it is setting the air conditioner on low in the RV. Of course, there's a slight problem. We do not have an RV. We do not even have a tent that fits. On our three-day trip to this gorgeous getaway, the five of us camped in a tent I found on a clearance table—a tent that slept three of us comfortably. Now, we've always been a close-knit family, but this was pushing it. Crammed into four sleeping bags, the rain pounding inches from our noses, and me too cheap to buy air mattresses, we groaned in agony as I told stories of the good old days, back when men were men and their wives were tired of it.

"Kids, did I ever tell you about the time wolves carried away my mother-in-law?" I asked before being pushed out the tent flap by my dear wife, whose sense of humor had vanished at the stroke of midnight. "On second thought, perhaps it was your Uncle Ivan," I yelled from outside the tent, standing up and whacking my head on a tree branch.

The next morning as I drove along at 55, nursing a welt that bore a startling resemblance to Mount Saint Helens, my wife reached over and gently patted my knee. "Honey," she said, in a voice that warns of things to come, "You are the cheapest person I have ever been married to."

"Wait a minute," I said. "That's not fair. I know cheaper people. For example, there's…um…well, there's Bill."

"How cheap is he?"

"He goes to cafeterias and pretends he's eating so he can fill his pockets with ketchup packets."

"That's not cheap, that's theft."

"Well, I'm not all that bad."

"Oh yes you are, Philip Ronald Callaway. And right now you will pull over to that Wal-Mart, where we will buy air mattresses, or tonight we'll see what the wolves do with *you!*"

"Honey," I asked, "is something troubling you?"

That night, as the children snored comfortably on their $5 air mattresses, Ramona and I argued about the trouble with cheapskates.

"Are we in debt?" I asked defensively. "Have we been spending money before making it?"

"No," replied Ramona, "But are we balanced? Are we generous? Are we holding things loosely?"

I let out a soft fake snore.

"Phil," she said, "you're so cheap, you bought air mattresses for everyone but yourself."

"If I promise to quit being so cheap," I said, "will you let me share yours?"

"Okay."

And she did.

The Stuff of Earth

As you can tell, one of Ramona's virtues is patience, something I continue to help her practice. On the cheapest trip we ever took, our disagreements centered solely on money. And, though it pains me to admit it, I was wrong approximately one hundred percent of the time.

During early morning walks along an Oregon beach, I began to realize this. Each morning as the sun rose, I read a chapter from the Gospel of Matthew and then strolled a few miles thinking about it. But mostly, I must admit, I thought about the condo and an upcoming interview in Atlanta. And I longed for a little more luxury in my life. After reading Matthew 6 one morning, I noticed Jesus' command: "You cannot serve both God and Money." *Obviously a command for the wealthy,* I thought as I sauntered down the beach, mentally calculating the gas mileage we'd been getting on the trip.

Then it hit me harder than that tree branch: Jesus wasn't just talking to the wealthy. He was talking to people like me. You see, even a penny held close enough to the eye can block our view of him. It doesn't have to be much, but if it's where I fix my eyes, I will miss what's most important.

"Lord," I prayed, "Help me be content wherever I am. Help me hold the stuff of earth loosely. Help me worship only you."

We said goodbye to the condo with a view, and as the rain began to fall on the last night of our vacation, found ourselves crammed once again into that crowded tent. We listened to some robins singing their children to sleep, and when everything was finally quiet, I asked the kids, "What did you like most about this trip? The condo? The sand castles? The ocean?"

Their answer took me by surprise. All three agreed: It was camping in a three-man tent.

"Dad, tell us about the wolf and Gramma," asked Stephen.

"You wouldn't dare," warned my wife. And I'm pleased to tell you, I didn't.

"When I was your age, I did something horrible," I began.

"What was it?"

"I stole some money from a friend of mine. His name was Willie, and he's a lawyer now…"

With money in your pocket, you are wise, and you are handsome, and you sing well too.

JEWISH PROVERB

28

The Beggar and the Billionaire

For a northern kid like me, Atlanta is hot in July. Like opening the oven door and poking your head in to see if the bread is done. As my plane touches down, I pack up a book I've been reading and step into the Georgia night. The taxi driver talks of weather and baseball's Braves, but my mind is haunted by a question the book has raised: "If grace is so amazing, why don't followers of Jesus show more of it?"

It is midnight when I arrive at my hotel, anxious for air conditioning. A smiling employee informs me that my "guaranteed room reservation" is no longer guaranteed.

"But I phoned ahead twice to ensure my reservations," I tell her angrily.

"I'm sorry," she says. "Some guests have stayed longer than expected. We're sending you to another hotel." Handing me $15 for a taxi, she listens to my response. It is anything but graceful.

The taxi bill comes to $10, and I pocket what's left, small consolation for the fact that I have been dumped in a darker area of town. Closing the hotel room curtains tight against beggars and bums, I push my luggage against the door and sit down to prepare for tomorrow's business, a grueling schedule that includes conducting a magazine interview with the first billionaire I've ever met.

Growing up, I somehow learned to view the wealthy with suspicion.

After all, the love of money was the root of all kinds of evil, wasn't it? And who could love money more than the man with lots of it? I begin writing out questions for tomorrow's interview. They come fast: Jesus said it was easier for a camel to squeeze through the eye of a needle than for a rich man to enter the kingdom of heaven. How come? And how does a billionaire live a rich life? I've always heard that rich people are miserable.

Outside on the darkened street, beggars look for an outstretched hand. As I drift off, I find myself wondering how I could get just a small handout from the billionaire.

After a few restless hours of sleep, I peek through the curtains. The streets are swept clean of beggars now, but the early morning sun makes the shabby buildings seem darker than the night before. I can't help thinking of the contrast between where I am and where I'm going.

Breakfast is toast and juice, and soon, under the watchful eye of his two assistants, I'm shaking hands with one of the wealthiest Christians on earth. A giant in the investment world, Robert Van Kampen was the pioneer of the insured mutual fund and founder and financial backer of the Scriptorium, the world's largest private collection of biblical manuscripts. He manages six companies with investments of over $70 billion, a figure I can't quite wrap my mind around. (A calculator would be no help. Most run out of digits. Doodling tells me that it's seventy thousand million-dollar bills.)

His opening remarks surprise me. "Don't be alarmed if I don't make it through this interview," he smiles, tapping a small heart rate monitor. "I have to check this thing every few minutes now. Doctor's orders, you know." He tells me of his recurring health problems. "Some things money can't buy."

"What *can* it buy?" I ask him.

"Well, when your motive is right, when God is number one, you'd be surprised what money can do."

"Like what?"

"Ten years ago I was shown a sixteenth-century Bible whose owner was killed for possessing it. It still had his bloodstains on it. This made such an impact on me that I bought the Bible and decided to commit myself to the collection and preservation of early manuscripts. The one thing I would die for is the preservation of God's truth. Money has helped me have a part in that."

"What would you say has made your life rich?"

He hesitates for a few moments. "Giving money away. I've found that you can never outgive God. If you give to get, chances are you won't get a dime. If you're giving out of a heart of gratitude for what God has given you, God turns around and blesses you. I've made some huge errors. I've lost more money in a year than some countries make. But the Lord makes it up to you if your motive is right. My life is a story of grace. I started with nothing, and I've been incredibly successful. God has trusted me with these funds, and he could take them away at any moment. To the best of my ability, I want to be trustworthy with what he's given me. We're not here long. God rewards our faithfulness whether we have a little or a lot."

He stops to check the monitor. "How do Christians treat you?" I ask.

"It's funny," he says. "Nobody likes a successful businessman, especially if he's a Christian. The only people who like you are the ones you're giving money to. Most people who get to know me now have an agenda. That's why some of my best friends are people I knew before I was successful. They liked me then. They like me now. I get so many requests from people for money..."

"That's why I came to see you," I say, laughing a little too loudly.

That night as I arrive at my hotel, a homeless man calls out for my attention: "Hey, man, why you walk on by? Why you treat me like garbage?"

I stop, perhaps unwisely.

"I'm sorry," I say. "I didn't mean to—" He holds out a free pass to the Gentleman's Club, a nude show just down the street. I show him my wedding ring. "I'm a Christian," I say, "and it's tough enough on business trips without you tempting me, man."

We laugh together. He can't stop apologizing. "I'm a Christian, too," he says, tossing a cigarette. "And…I'm ashamed."

A policeman stops and gets out of his car. "Everything all right?" he asks in a Southern drawl. I assure him that it is.

"They ain't used to no one talkin' to us," the beggar tells me as the police car pulls away.

For the next half hour I sit on the curb, listening to his story. Loss of job, loss of family, drugs, alcohol, depression, attempted suicide. "Last night I slept behind them garbage cans," he points. His breath causes me to inch away. "A rat bit me in the knuckle…right here."

Not knowing what to believe, I ask him, "So, what would Jesus say to you?"

"Oh man…he'd say that he loves me. I sit over by them garbage cans most nights, and I don't sing so hot, but I sing, 'Amazing grace, how sweet the sound that saved a wretch like me…' God's grace. It's the only thing that's got me through."

The police car coasts slowly by, and I sit quietly, reflecting on his words. Reflecting on my tendency to judge too quickly.

Then I pull the $5 from my pocket and add a few more. "I don't know how you'll spend this," I say, "but that's not up to me."

After teaching me a series of handshakes, he listens as I urge him to try to get his job back. Then we part ways. Sometimes his words still echo in my ears: "God's grace. It's the only thing that's got me through."

Not long after my taped interview with Mr. Van Kampen, I learned that he had died at the age of 60 while awaiting a heart transplant. The last sentences he says on the tape are these: "We're not here long. God rewards our faithfulness whether we have a little or a lot."

There, but for the grace of God, goes John Bradford.

JOHN BRADFORD (1510–1555)

29

Jim Bakker and Me

When I was informed by a Nashville publicist that Jim Bakker wanted to talk with me, I must admit, I wasn't impressed. The sad truth is, I didn't much like the disgraced televangelist. Not so many years ago you could hardly bump into a tabloid or flip on a TV set without sharing in his disgrace. I'd even found myself laughing at jokes about the makeup his wife, Tammy Faye, wore. And making up a few of my own.

Would I like to talk to Jim Bakker? No thank you.

I knew his story all too well. Notorious for achieving the American dream as leader of the multimillion-dollar empires Heritage USA, *The PTL Club,* and the PTL Television Network, Bakker seemed to revel in his prestige, his power, and the adoration of millions. A premiere proponent of the prosperity gospel, he preached an upbeat message of optimism, health, and wealth.

But his world caved in when a sexual encounter with Jessica Hahn, a church secretary from New York, became international news. The loss of his reputation was only the beginning. Convicted of mail and wire fraud for fund-raising efforts at PTL, the former confidant of presidents found himself sentenced to 45 years in a federal prison. Released after five years, Jim Bakker had just finished his memoirs, *I Was Wrong,* when his publicist called.

"Why won't you talk with him?" she asked. "He's doing very few interviews."

"I don't know," I replied, pausing. "I guess I'm pretty cynical...how much money is he making from this book?"

"He can't receive any royalties because of taxes and litigation fees."

"Hmm...well, sure, I'll talk to him." I knew the conversation would be an interesting one. But I would never put it into print.

A few days later I found myself conversing with a soft-spoken man, very different from the television persona I remember, one who had lost his wife, his dignity, and every penny he had. Barbara Walters had just left his house after a tear-filled interview, but I felt little emotion as I asked him why he wrote the book.

"I want my children, my grandchildren, and the people who supported and watched me for twenty-five years to understand what I learned in prison—that my previous philosophy of life was flawed," he said. "I once taught people not to pray 'Thy will be done,' when they want a new car, but just to claim it. I preached that God wanted everybody to be rich and prosperous, with no pain and no problems—a Pollyanna gospel. But the prosperity gospel doesn't make much sense when you're locked up in prison. As I studied the Bible there, I was appalled that I could have been so wrong, and I was deeply grateful that God had not struck me dead as a false prophet. I had taught people to fall in love with money. The deceitfulness of riches and the lust for other things had choked out the Word of God in my life and in the lives of my family members and coworkers. God does not promise riches or prosperity, but he promises to never leave or forsake us, no matter what pain or trial we're going through."

"What changed your mind?"

"The words of Jesus. For two solid years in prison, I read and reread every word he said. I wrote them out countless times and studied them in the Greek. As I began to study Jesus, I didn't find him saying anything good about money. In Luke 6:24 he says, 'Woe to you who are rich.' Matthew 6:19 says, 'Do not store up for yourselves treasures on earth.' How could I be telling people to get rich?"

The reason was simple. Bakker preached selectively, skipping over verses or rationalizing them away. *Surely the love of money couldn't be the root of evil,* he told himself. *Surely it was something more terrible, like murder or hatred.* He says he preached "long-horned sermons"—a point here, a point there, and lots of bull in between.

"I would take a verse from the Old Testament, a verse from the New, and put a lot of Jim Bakker in between. I took success books and put Scriptures to them. I would get off on what's wrong with the government, on scaring people about this and that, but what people needed was the Word of God. In Matthew 7, Jesus said, 'Many will say to me on that day, "Lord, Lord, did we not prophesy in your name, and in your name drive out demons and perform many miracles?" And he will tell them, 'I never knew you. Away from me, you evildoers!' The Greek word for *knew* means an intimate relationship. Christ is not interested in our prophesies or our huge bank accounts. I knew rich men who prophesied and lived like the devil. Jesus will say, 'I never knew them.' He has never had an intimate relationship with them. I should have taught people to fall in love with Jesus rather than the trappings."

At this point in our conversation, I began questioning my initial decision about printing the interview. "What is it about prison that radically transforms so many?" I asked.

"In prison you are forced to take a Sabbath. I had five years of Sabbaths. In a real way God brought me to prison to die, but not physically. He allowed me to be incarcerated so I could die to myself. In prison I came to the end of Jim Bakker."

"How are you different from before you went to prison?"

He answered softly, "Oh…I'm so different. I feel totally unworthy to stand in the pulpit. I don't have the ambitions I once had. I just live one day at a time. I want to be where God wants me. I don't have a reputation, so I don't have to prove anything to anybody. I can minister to anyone. Jesus could sit in the marketplace with a prostitute or at Matthew's house with criminals. He made himself of no reputation. It's a marvelous place to be. I don't have a lot of bills, just my rent and utilities and groceries. I used to have to raise a million dollars every two days. That's pretty nice not to have over your head."

"Do you blame your wife for divorcing you?"

"I was facing forty-five years in prison. She was someone who needed someone there every hour of every day to be told she's loved. I carried her. I pampered her. I babied her for thirty years, so much of it is my fault, I guess. I take responsibility for the divorce. I went to prison. I made wrong decisions."

Quickly he changed the subject, telling me of the joy of his life—his grandchildren. "The title of this book is not what you want for your memoirs; not what you'd like to pass on to your grandchildren. But my children are very gracious. They should be bitter and away from God, but both of them are serving him."

"Can God still use someone who has failed?" I asked.

He told of a cold January morning when he was summoned from his cell. Sick with the flu and filthy from cleaning toilets, he reluctantly accompanied a guard to the warden's office. There a visitor was waiting.

It was Billy Graham.

"As I walked through the door, he turned toward me and opened his arms wide. Immediately I felt total acceptance and love. I wanted to run into his arms like a little boy would run into his daddy's arms. We talked for a while, and when he left he told me he'd be praying for me. I knew then that God loved me, that God could use me again. That's the grace of God."

"God has forgiven you. Do you ever wonder if Christians will?"

His voice grew even quieter. "Ministers told me that God didn't love me. So many Christians have harbored hatred toward me. I felt God hated me. But he said he will never, never leave me. The first thing I do at every service I go to is ask forgiveness of the people. The Bible says unless you forgive, you will not be forgiven. There are so many Scriptures in the Bible about judging and not judging. If you judge, you'll be judged the same way. If you don't forgive, you'll not be forgiven. Unforgiveness kills the person who doesn't forgive."

"I need to ask your forgiveness too," I said. "I…well, I never really liked Jim Bakker."

"I didn't either." He offered a smile. "But God did."

"Why would God allow you to lose everything and end up in prison?"

"Because he loves me. Those he loves he chastens. The Bible says the trial of your faith is more precious than gold. I had been telling people that if they had problems, it was because they had sin in their lives. I was teaching them how *not* to 'become gold.' It was God's grace that took me to jail. In prison, a young bank robber asked me, 'Why does God hate me?' When I told him of God's love, he wasn't impressed. But months later he told me I was right. He said, 'I'd be dead if God hadn't intervened in my life.' If I would have kept on going, I would have ended up in a mental institution or at least totally burned-out. I would not go back to the way things were for anything. God used the circumstances of losing PTL to bring me to a place of genuine brokenness, repentance, and surrender. It hurt. And the losses my family and I have endured have been many and irreplaceable. But in the light of eternity, it will be worth it all."

Although the final chapter has yet to be written, I can't help but be reminded of another humbled sinner, one who failed his country and failed his God—King David. In both cases, the sinner found what amazes every one of us who falls and gets back up—God's amazing grace. It is truly the most wonderful gift that money can't buy.

And one I would need during the next chapter of my life.

Wealth is any income that is at least one hundred dollars a year more than the income of one's wife's sister's husband.

H.L. Mencken

30

Making Life Rich...with Money

Back when Muhammad Ali ruled the boxing world, he was stopped for speeding on his way to a title fight. When the police officer pulled him over and informed Ali's limo driver that the ticket would cost them $100, the famous boxer handed his driver $200.

"Give this to him," he commanded. "And tell him we're coming back this way."

There's no doubt about it, money has its advantages. Of course, it won't buy you happiness, it won't buy you love, and it certainly won't buy what it used to, but I'd be foolish to say that money won't buy anything useful. As the British politician and businessman Lord Mancroft once said, "Money, if it does not bring you happiness, will at least help you to be miserable in comfort."

Here are a few of the things money can and cannot buy:

Nice houses, but not a home.

A fancy bed, but not a peaceful sleep.

Companions, but not friends.

Food, but not satisfaction.

Sex, but not love.

New cars, but not safety.

Pills, but not health.

Fun, but not fulfillment.

Sun-filled vacations, but not peace.

In my survey of almost 1000 people, I asked them what good things money had bought them. A handful were confused by the question. Twenty-three said "nothing." The highest percentage (67 percent) mentioned their houses. From there the list looked like this:

vacations with family (39%)

an education (22%)

medical care (19%)

the chance to give it away (18%)

a car (17%)

a wedding ring (13%)

mission trips (12%)

food (10%)

a camera (9%)

a musical instrument (9%)[2]

Without a doubt, money is a blessing. I don't meet a lot of people who can live without food, clothing, or shelter, and I find very few stores that exchange these items for pine needles. Money comes in handy. It is useful.

After surviving five horrible months imprisoned by North Vietnamese soldiers in the worst conditions imaginable, my friend and hero Lloyd Opell said, "I appreciated food as never before. I rhapsodized over cabbage and soliloquized over a good turnip. Food rocks!"

I have been in countries where people are dying daily for lack of these blessings. And I have heard Westerners piously mock money while enjoying the highest standard of living in human history. Lloyd told me, "God does not call us to be antimaterialist, but to worship at the feet of him who has created our universe and shared its wealth with us so unstintingly."

I have always loved the words *my* and *mine.* "Hey, that's mine!" My baseball glove. My bike. My car. My house.

But when our financial fortunes changed, my questions began to change too. I had to ask, whose stuff is this? Are my time, talents, money, and things really mine? Or do they belong to God?

Whose Stuff Is It?

Let's suppose that I call your house to tell you what I've been up to this week. "Hey, I'm out in California," I say. "I rented a car at LAX. One of those Mercedes-Benz SL-class roadsters. It's pretty cool, but a few things bugged me about it. The alabaster white color was too... too white. So on Monday I had a body shop redo it in Iridium Silver Metallic."

"Say what?" you stammer.

"And the V-8 just didn't have the pep, so on Tuesday I had a mechanic pop in a 5980 cc V-12 with an overhead cam and three valves per cylinder. You should hear this puppy rev."

"You what?"

"And the black leather seats are too hot when the top is down, so on Wednesday I had them replaced with beige. It goes better with my pants."

I think I can anticipate your response: "I thought you said you rented it."

"I did."

"But how long are you staying there?"

"A week."

"Have you lost your mind, Callaway?"

And of course I would have to answer yes. But I wonder sometimes how much of our time, talents, and cash are spent on stuff that will fade as quickly as a one-week car rental. I wonder if we really believe that our lives are vapors, that as James says, we appear for a little while and then vanish away.[3] We get so time locked, so sure that this is all at least a little bit permanent, that we can't think straight.

Those with aging parents have seen them go from big houses filled with stuff to sparsely furnished apartments or nursing homes. Buy now and one thing is sure: Later comes fast. The things we coveted yesterday will vanish in tomorrow's yard sale. Everyone in a nursing home who can still speak will say the same thing: "The years go by so fast." And you still can't buy saddlebags for your coffin.

Whether we have a little or a lot, our success in life could hinge on our answer to one solitary question: Is this stuff mine, or is it God's? Did I earn this because I'm so amazing, because I worked so hard and achieved so much? Or are these things gifts of grace, entrusted to me for some greater purpose?

If we are rich in stuff, we are instructed not to be arrogant or to put our hope in wealth, but to put our hope in God, who richly provides us with everything for our enjoyment.[4]

Our lives change course when we simply realize that everything we have is God's and we are simply called to be thankful stewards of his assets—managers, if you will—enjoying the gifts God gives, using them for his eternal purposes, and doing so with a grin.

On TV and radio, in magazines and newspapers, get-rich-quick schemes abound. Telemarketers inform us that the future is ours with a few wise investments. In the last six months I have been approached on numerous occasions by people—many of them Christians—with dollar signs in their eyes. "Phil, this product has really changed our lives," they tell me. "We'd love to sign you up to sell it." Of course I have nothing against making a living, but I must admit that I'm alarmed at the ease with which we put so much stock in the latest product or fad. Of course I support the wise handling of our finances. Retirement savings plans are fine, but they will never secure our future.

Jesus had much to say about money (about one-fifth of his recorded words, in fact) because he knew of our propensity to fall in love with it. To worship it. To find our security in it. And so he challenged us to "store up for yourselves treasures in heaven, where moth and rust do not destroy, and where thieves do not break in and steal" (Matthew 6:20). In 1 Peter 1:3-5, the apostle Peter talked about the only guaranteed and lasting investment: "In his great mercy he has given us new birth into a living hope through the resurrection of Jesus Christ from the dead, and into an inheritance that can never perish, spoil or fade—kept in heaven for you."

Our possessions are a trust from God. What we clutch tightly, we lose. What we place in His hands, we will possess for eternity.

Perhaps money is a bit like sunlight. You can welcome it and enjoy it and be warmed by it. But in the end, you cannot bottle the stuff. You can reflect it, though, and store it in a divine bank account with heavenly interest.

What If You Won?

At least once a week I stand impatiently in line behind people who are playing the lottery, and I wonder what kind of people they would be if they won. Would this be a better world? Would they have better lives? Would they really enrich the lives of others?

Like many of my generation, I have journeyed from having little to being entrusted with a lot. And I have discovered something profound: More money just makes you more of what you already were.

Are you greedy now? Get more money and you'll be greedier.

Are you a whiner now? Trust me, you'll have more to whine about then.

Are you vengeful now? Money will give you more opportunities to seek vengeance.

But if you are generous, if you hold what you have today in an open hand, more money will increase the opportunities to be even more openhanded.

Perhaps God is merciful enough to not bless us with it until he knows he can trust us with it.

Openhanded Doug

The world abounds with examples of those who have much, but it is in painfully short supply of those who live with open hands.

I applaud friends of mine like the founder of Action International, Doug Nichols, who has sacrificially served God and others around the world. He often takes a reduced monthly salary because he meets people who need his money more than he does.

One day Doug told me of the time he and his staff of almost 200 in the Philippines were visited by Franklin Graham, son of Billy Graham. On the way to the airport, Franklin, who never shies away from telling it like it is, said, "You know Doug, I have been all over the world, and I've ridden in every kind of vehicle imaginable, but this car of yours is the worst I have ever been in! Where did you get this thing?"

They laughed together as Doug told him horror stories of the time the steering wheel came completely off and the time the gearshift slipped out. As Doug pulled Franklin's bags from the car at the airport, Franklin said, "Doug, all joking aside, I would like to mention something. I feel you are working your people too hard."

"You're right," agreed Doug.

"When was the last time you took your team on a break?"

"A *what?*"

"A break, a retreat, a time of fellowship and refreshment."

Doug was ashamed. "Never."

Franklin reached into his pocket and did better than Muhammad Ali. He pulled out 20 100-dollar bills and said, "This is a gift from Samaritan's Purse."

Doug was able to take the whole team, including their families, for a three-day retreat, where they enjoying each other's company, prayed, rested, and played.

For those with money, it is the love of the stuff that will kill you. Lavishing it on others can make you rich.

Ever wonder about those people who spend $2 apiece on those little bottles of Evian water? Try spelling Evian backward.

George Carlin

31

How to Save $11,000 a Year

Recently a lady confessed to me that she was such a tightwad, she used to steal lightbulbs from restaurant restrooms. I said, "Honey, you have to stop that." I'm kidding. It wasn't really my wife.

But regardless of how much we earn, cheapness can linger. I do not recommend being a skinflint. But we can nurture some simple behaviors that allow us to save money we can use to celebrate and give. Much of what we spend is simply gone without thought, enjoyment, or memories, so here are 24 ways to help you to save major bucks and savor the right things.

1. Hit the mute button during commercials. Advertisers spend millions creating necessities for us and convincing us that we are miserable. We're not. They are liars and should have their mouths washed out with Tide.[5]

2. Buy a lottery ticket once every three million years.

3. Eat out less. Restaurant food is higher in salt, fat, preservatives, grease, and price. Besides, a stranger prepares it. Nowhere does the Bible forbid throwing a bag of carrots, a few tomatoes, and a saltshaker into the backseat and letting the kids munch on them. Of course, if you must eat out…

4. Split a plate. You don't have to wait until you're old enough to

order from the senior's menu. Start now. Most portions in American restaurants will feed a family of 34 anyway. In fact, no one has finished a meal in a Texas restaurant since John Candy wolfed down the "Old 96er" (96 ounces of fat and gristle) in *The Great Outdoors.*

5. Write up a shopping list and stick with it.

6. Car shopping? Take a mechanic out for a nice dinner. Then pay him his going rate to accompany you to a car auction. Buy a three-year-old "preloved" vehicle. During the course of your working career, you will save more than $200,000 this way (minus the mechanic's meals).

7. Bring back the Easy Load Crock Pot. You can let stuff simmer for weeks in these things. Ah, the aroma. Ah, the taste. Ah, the savings.

8. Never shop when you're hungry. Or angry. Or depressed. Or while having hot flashes.

9. Don't buy something only because you have a coupon.

10. Eat lunch, but don't *do* lunch. Spending $7 each working day on lunch can set you back $1750 a year. So stuff a lunch in your briefcase. (Remember it's there, and do not set anything heavy on it. I have done this.)

11. Avoid retail.

12. Order water. Most restaurants do not charge for this unless you order it in bottles labeled *Oui Le Riche.* Those who study such things tell us that a can of pop costs 2500 times as much as a glass of water.

13. Avoid "Don't Pay Until March 2384" signs.

14. Here is my secret to the good life: Phil's Homemade Fruit Smoothie for Nonalcoholics. Buy these at a mall and...well, you can't. These are only made by someone who loves you.

> 1 can genuine mango juice
>
> strawberry yogurt
>
> chopped ice (add or subtract according to outside temperature)
>
> 1 orange (remove rinds unless you enjoy them)

1 cup milk (use before expiry date)

2 bananas (set aside peels for pranks)

Blend well. Fills four non-teenagers at about 65 cents each.

15. Have a garden, regardless of how small.

16. Brew iced tea. Pop three tea bags and a fat lemon wedge in 2 quarts of water and microwave for 10 minutes on high. Stir in some sugar until the sampler stops puckering. For optimum results, leave it in the sun a few hours. For memorable results, store it in the back of the fridge for 12 months.

17. Use wallpaper as gift wrap. It looks better, and the right sale will bring you big savings. Don't lick it, though, or leave it in the rain. Want to save even more? Wrap gifts in the Sunday funnies.

18. Forget $5.99 greeting cards. Buy blank ones in bulk. People read your handwriting and skim everything else anyway.

19. Your clothes will fade less if you wash them inside out.

20. Acquaint yourself with a classy secondhand clothing store. It's not an oxymoron.

21. Spend time going through your bills each month. Don't be afraid to challenge bank, phone, or credit card statements.

22. Be generous with your time. Babysit, houseclean, or spontaneously wash a friend's car. The shock value will be priceless.

23. Moviepool. Let friends know when you've rented a movie. Do not rent it to them; lend it. Better yet, invite them over.

24. Sit long. Talk much. Eat dessert.

He is richest who is content with the least.

Socrates

32

What Money Can Buy

For six years, an Indiana couple looked on the ground everywhere they went. They didn't make many new friends, but the habit paid off. "We now have $400 in a container," they say. Craig Davidson of Phoenix has them beat. He has found $5170 while jogging. His wife verifies the claim. "Craig runs a lot more than the average jogger," she said. Perhaps he will spend some of it on a treadmill.

When I was about five, I found a quarter on a sidewalk one morning (probably made more than my dad that day!), and before rushing to the candy store, I ran home to show it to my mother. "I'm gonna look for money everywhere I go now," I told her, gasping for breath. My wise mother sat me down and told me a story about a man who found $5 in a gutter and spent the rest of his life looking for more. According to my mother, he never saw the trees. He never saw the flowers. He never saw the birds. In fact, he missed a hundred rainbows and a thousand sunsets. All he saw was gutters. "I hope you enjoy that candy, Philip," she said, "but remember...always look a little higher."

Here are the stories of some folks who have learned the joy of looking a little higher. These people are learning what a buck can (and cannot) buy.

"We were poor seminary students with two young daughters, and we dearly wanted a son. After interviewing with a private adoption agency that placed children ages three or older with no fees attached, we were approved to adopt in August. In October we received a call asking if we would adopt a 17-day-old boy. Because he was a baby, he came with fees totaling $3600. The agency knew we had little cash, so they offered to waive their fee, cutting the total in half. Of course, we didn't have the $1800 either. Our care group at the church gave us a money tree shower and raised $600. We made a down payment, and the agency allowed us to pay $100 a month until we paid off the debt. Our 'baby mortgage' payments lasted a year, and our baby will soon be 26. He's priceless!"

"A few years ago our church sent a container of clothes to the Ukraine. Our family wanted to spend $100, so we found a store that gave us a good deal on a $100 worth of wool work socks. Giving money away has made my life richer."

"Sometime in my childhood I developed a 'bucket list,' though I never associated it with my eventual demise. I figured I'd do the hard stuff when I was young and save the gourmet tour of Southern France for some far distant time—like when I was 50! In my twenties, I sat on the Great Wall of China, paddled on the Amazon, and visited my homeland of Scotland. Now that I'm in my fifties, I've been to Africa twice, though I still haven't done the gourmet tour of Southern France! I've never regretted spending money to see the world; it's broadened my horizons and given me an interest in what's happening in other countries. It's also made me a tolerant parent of one son and his wife, who have made similar investments in wandering."

"Five years ago my husband and I had 11 credit cards and a debt of $100,000. Today we are debt free. For us the steps to financial freedom were simple but not always easy. First we quit spending more than we were making. Then we had a melt-down-our-plastic party. Then we paid God first (about 15 percent), paid ourselves next (putting away 10 percent each month), and paid the bills with what was left. We've had to downsize our dreams a little, but the nightmares have gone away. We've even had enough to give to some needy friends. Our lives are richer far because of it."

"In my hurry to make it to work this morning, I ignored icy conditions, slid into a curb, and readjusted my truck's alignment. That was just the start of a horrible day. When I arrived home, my youngest greeted me at a decibel level only a parent could appreciate: 'Daddy, Daddy, Daddy.' Then I remembered my New Year's resolution: 'I will look for the wealth of things God has blessed me with even in the midst of hard times.' I also recalled that when Matthew Henry was robbed, he wrote in his diary, 'Let me be thankful…first, because I was never robbed before…second, because although they took my wallet they did not take my life…third, because although they took my all, it was not much…and fourth, because it was I who was robbed, not I who did the robbing.'"

"I'm a fan of money because it paid the adoption expenses for two sons and heart surgery for our third son."

"We're moving across town to the wrong side of the tracks this week, into the Somali slums here in Nairobi. These past two years our lives have been richer because of these refugees. We have fed, clothed, and prayed with people who every day suffer more than I thought anyone could. I've discovered that life is harder than I'd ever imagined, but I have also discovered that God is bigger and better than I'd ever imagined. We left a comfortable home in North America to offer the hope of eternity to suffering people. This has made our lives rich indeed."

"I am a student, and I am many thousands of dollars in debt. I do not have good prospects for a high-paying job. I do not own a home, a car, a dog, or a white picket fence. But if I were granted a wish, I do not think I would ask for anything. I have a loving wife and soon-to-be-born child. I am clothed, fed, and housed. I am doing what I most love to do. I have a network of caring and supportive relationships through friends and family. And I am an heir of God's grace. He satisfies my desires with good things. He has seen me thus far, and he will see me home."

"A year ago we decided to quit eating out so much and use the money to support a needy child through Compassion International. We keep her picture in our dining room and pray for her almost every night. Our daughters write her letters and consider her a part of our extended family. It's tough not to feel rich when you're giving money away."

"I noticed the other day that a widow in our town is working two jobs to make ends meet. I'm able to make some extra money, so we've started sending her what we can. She doesn't know about it, but our kids sure do. It's probably the only family secret we have. Every time I come back from speaking, the kids want to know...can we give more money to our widow friend?"

"A few days after Jill was born, my wife and I were carrying her out of the hospital to take her home. An elderly man from our church was pacing the lobby. His wife was in the hospital dying of cancer, and he spent most of his time with her. Smiling, he pressed a $20 bill into my hand. 'My wife and I were never able to have children,' he said. 'But we hear you'll be needing lots of this. God bless you.' Four years have passed, and he is a widower now. Whenever we see him sitting alone at church, our family sits beside him. I'm sure our kids are a little noisy sometimes, but he doesn't seem to mind. And one of them has even started calling him Grandpa. She's his favorite—our four-year-old, Jill."

"The best investment I ever made was in the engagement ring that bolstered my courage to ask my girlfriend to marry me 32 years ago. She said yes. At $65, it was a pretty good investment."

"After I had been climbing the corporate ladder for many years, my marriage was failing. Then the company I had given so much to went bankrupt. To thank me for my years of dedication, they even bounced my last two paychecks. I've never been one to run from a challenge, so I decided to rebuild my home with God's help—one day at a time. My wife and I just celebrated our twenty-third anniversary. Our son gave me a card thanking me for being his father and showing him how to be a man. In that moment all the effort was worth it. Without love there are only houses. Without my family I would have no home. I'm the richest man alive when I'm just Dad."

And finally, this from my brother-in-law Jim Nikkel, whose wife is battling Huntington's disease: "They say that money won't buy you love, but my love has cost me a lot of money. And it's the best money I've ever spent." Thank God for faithful guys like Jim.

Part Five

Rich People Leave the Right Stuff Behind

My friend Ron travels the world with Franklin Graham. One day Franklin told him about a visit to America's deadliest prison, Louisiana State Penitentiary in Angola, where the warden, Burl Cain, offered him a tour. "All these men will die here," Cain said. "Of the 5108 inmates, 3700 are serving life sentences, and the others average 88 years each."

When Franklin was shown one of the simple, birch plywood caskets the inmates are buried in, he was struck by its simplicity and beauty. "This is symbolic of my parents' lives," he said. "This is what they would want to be buried in. I'd like to order two." Cain was astonished and offered to build with richer materials. Franklin refused. "I want them built just as if they were for inmates," he insisted. They cost about $200 each. "We're humbled they would use a coffin built by our inmates," said Cain.

A few days after celebrating her eighty-seventh birthday, Ruth Graham's family stood around her bed singing "Great Is Thy Faithfulness," and as they sang the doxology, she was free at last, passing into the presence of Christ. Ruth Bell Graham was buried in a simple wooden box handcrafted by death-row inmates.

When we leave this earth, we won't take much. But we do leave footprints everywhere we go. Rich people pause to ponder what it will take to leave footprints worth following.

Here are a few stories of the things we leave behind.

The measure of a man's true wealth is not in what he kept but what he gave; not what he made but what he left. There is no legacy so rich and powerful as a godly example.

The law tells me how crooked I am. Grace comes along and straightens me out.

D.L. Moody

33

Up in Smoke

I grew up in a rather conservative community. How conservative? Well, some in our church felt we shouldn't associate with the Amish because they dressed a bit too flashy. Of course, I'm stretching things a little, but the truth is, regardless of which way the wind blew, we leaned a little to the right.

Sundays we worshipped and slept (sometimes simultaneously), Wednesdays we faithfully attended prayer meeting (unless my prayers were answered and my father forgot!), and Friday evenings we gathered around campfires to sing, "It only takes a spark to get a fire going" (unless Basic Youth Conflicts was in town).

We did not play cards (except Rook), attend movies (except *The Hiding Place*), or yell "Shoot!" (except during church basketball games). Most of our parents enjoyed George Beverly Shea's music until the percussion section got carried away, and we were taught to dance only when shot at with live ammunition.

I almost feel guilty mentioning it, but I had a great deal of fun growing up this way. Oh sure, there were negative side effects. For instance, there was the memory loss. And there was, uh...I can't remember the other thing. Seriously, certain side effects do linger. For one thing, I grew up experiencing ample guilt. For years I woke up with an Elmer-Fudd-like voice inside my head saying, *Hey you, you're guilty...GUILTY!*

I also had the strong impression that following Jesus was an outward thing. Though I often heard that works weren't the ticket to heaven, we found out early that our actions gained us approval (or disapproval) down here. The result was a tendency to fake faith. It's not that hard. I excelled at it for decades.

I also grew up believing that God wanted me miserable. Don't ask me why. I guess I saw it in the faces of those who came to church looking like breakfast was a fruit cup of prunes and lemons sautéed in vinegar. God's will for my life, I thought, included serving him in the remotest part of India, married to the girl who sat at the front of our class squealing on everyone. And so, reluctant to trust God with everything I had, I decided to pursue adventure elsewhere.

You didn't have to look far in those days. For a mischievous child, it only took a spark to get a scandal going.

When I was ten, I invented recycling. I know it sounds improbable, but it's true. One August afternoon, a friend and I took a paper sack to our town's main street and placed in it every cigarette butt we could find. Loudly we proclaimed, "Boy, are these ever disgusting! Can you believe people actually smoke these things?" And passersby nodded their approval. Such good children, such conscientious children. There is hope for the next generation after all.

We smiled and curtsied and thanked them for their comments. Then we lugged the paper sack to our fort in the woods and recycled those cigarettes—every last one of them, right down to the filters. And unlike certain U.S. presidents, we inhaled. In fact, we recycled pretty much anything we could get our lips around that summer. Tea leaves, pencil shavings, cinnamon, cardboard, cow pies...you name it, we sat in the weeds and inhaled it.

One fine Wednesday our dreams came true. Discarded in a deserted ditch was the desire of our hearts: a package of filter-tipped cigarettes, unopened and beckoning. Stripping the plastic off, we divided the pack evenly—ten apiece—and sat in the tall weeds inhaling every last one of them, right down to the filters.

After staggering back to the nonsmoking zone, my friend was caught yellow-handed by his mother. But I was older and wiser. I knew that as ye smoke, so shall ye reek. Besides, I knew the punishment for smoking in our conservative community. My older brother Tim (now a Baptist minister) told me, "They catch you smoking, they cut your lips off."

So I slipped silently up to our medicine cabinet and found a can of spray deodorant. I finished it. Then I pulled out a full tube of toothpaste. I finished that too. Finally I was able to approach my parents.

"My, you smell nice, Son."

"Thank you," I said. "Thank you very much."

And that night I crawled into bed, a satisfied smile stuck to my face. *Boy, are you brilliant,* I thought. *No one will ever know.*

My mother entered the room then and sat on my bed, sniffing.

"How did it taste?" she asked.

"Uh...supper? It was great, Mom. Thank you very much."

"When I was a little girl," she continued, skipping nary a beat, "Grandpa let me smoke his pipe. I didn't much like it. How about you?"

She could have cut my lips off or preached to me or quoted Scripture. She could have reminded me that no amount of toothpaste or deodorant will cover our sins and that they really will find us out. She could have reminded me that the story doesn't end there, that because of what Jesus did on the cross, we don't have to hide. We can approach God, forever forgiven. Instead, she leaned over and kissed me gently on the forehead. "Smoking won't send you to hell, Son," she whispered. "It'll just make you smell like you've been there."

"Mom, how did you know?"

"Well," she said, tucking the covers in around my shoulders, "sometimes ten-year-old boys forget that their mothers have friends too."

And I heard my father's voice, coming from the bathroom. "Hey, has anyone seen the deodorant?"

Looking back on my childhood, I'm thankful for rules. I'm thankful I learned early about the consequences of sin. But I'm glad I was shown more. I'm glad I was shown such amazing grace.

I have thought of my mother's response often. It has come back to haunt me when called upon to forgive my children for engaging in some mind-numbingly juvenile activity. This grace is surely one of the keys to leaving the right footprints behind.

On the night I turned 35, I was tucking my ten-year-old son into bed. He looked at me and said, "Dad, you're half dead." I kissed the boy goodnight and then went across the hallway and removed him from the will. Actually, I stood there thinking about the shortness of my years. Psalm 90:10 (NLT) reminds us, "Seventy years are given to us! Some even live to eighty. But even the best years are filled with pain and trouble; soon they disappear, and we fly away."

I prayed that God would give me the strength to leave a lasting legacy of grace. And I prayed for my son, that he would discover early that rules are necessary, that Christians are human, and that God's will is the very best thing. I prayed that he would love the Lord Jesus with everything he's got. And I preached a little too. After telling him my smoking story, I pulled the blankets under his chin and said, "Breathe deeply of grace, Son. You'll find, as I have, that we travel a little lighter when God's grace carries us along."

A teacher affects eternity; he can never tell where his influence stops.

Henry Brooks Adams

34

One Flew over the Teacher's Desk

Well, it's been quite a week. On Wednesday the children brought home their report cards. On Thursday we went to see their teachers and beg for forgiveness. Sometimes at night, as we sit around the dinner table, I ask the kids, "So, what did you learn today?"

Almost without exception, they respond, "Nothing." Their report cards prove that they weren't lying.

People say that the world will never be a better place until children are an improvement on their parents, and I must admit that though my kids' marks leave a little to be desired, they are a dramatic improvement on mine.

One of the greatest ironies of my life is being asked to speak at teachers' conventions. You must understand that they used to spank me for speaking in class. In fact, to the best of my knowledge, I still hold the record for most whippings in a week at Prairie Elementary School. Please understand that I'm not proud of this. No siree. But let me tell you all about it.

I was homeschooled until the age of five, at which point my mother gave up on me and turned me over to the educational system. On my very first day of school, Leslie Kolibaba squealed on me for having my eyes open during prayer (yes, they prayed back then), and I have wondered for years how he knew. Teachers viewed me with suspicion from that day onward, and grown-ups soon grew tired of me. "Calm down," they'd say. Or "slow down," "settle down," "sit down," "simmer down," "climb down from there," and "lie down." They said that a lot at night. "If you don't lie down, I'll come down there, and you'll wish I hadn't gotten up." This is where it got confusing for me. In the morning they'd say, "wake up," "stand up," "dress up," "hurry up," "smarten up," "pick that up," "eat up," "buckle up," "shut up," and "grow up."

By third grade I was known as a kid who couldn't keep still, couldn't keep quiet, and couldn't keep from asking questions. I discovered that I could drive a grown-up completely nuts in three to five minutes with one powerful word: "Why?"

> Me: "Whatcha doin'?"
> Mr. Porr: "Weeding the corn."
> Me: "Why?"
> Mr. Porr: "Because if one organism occupies a particular space in an ecosystem, another organism cannot do so."
> Me: "Pardon me?"
> Mr. Porr: "Weeds choke the corn."
> Me: "Why?"
> Mr. Porr: "Because God cursed the ground, and we've got weeds."
> Me: "Why?"
> Mr. Porr (reaching for my neck): "Because mankind sinned and...would you like to know what it feels like to be choked?"
> Me: "Aaahhh!"

The questions I asked my teachers had less to do with horticulture and more to do with general annoyance: Why isn't *phonetic* spelled the way it sounds? Why doesn't glue stick to the inside of the bottle? Why is the word *abbreviation* so long? Why don't psychics win the lottery? Can fat people go skinny-dipping?

When they looked around their classrooms, they must have wondered whether us kids were learning anything at all. But the answer was obvious: no. As proof, here are a few things students have written on tests and essays over the years:

- Benjamin Franklin invented electricity by rubbing cats backward.
- Bach died from 1750 to the present.
- Queen Victoria was the longest queen. She sat on a thorn for 63 years.
- Socrates died from an overdose of wedlock.
- Christopher Columbus circumcised the earth with a 100-foot clipper.
- A man should have only one wife. This is called monotony.

Though I was sharp with my wit, my marks began slipping in kindergarten, and by the time I reached high school, I wished for all the world that I could quit.

To complicate matters, some strange teachers roamed the classrooms. One prided himself on addressing people by their birthdays. I was July 26. A friend of mine was May 3. "Hi, May 3," he'd say, walking past us in the hall. Or, "July 26, would you stand and read paragraph three from page 220?"[1]

Thankfully, we had other teachers too.

In tenth grade, I was standing at the drinking fountain, swapping jokes with friends when my English teacher, Mr. Bienert, tapped me on the shoulder. Taking me aside, he told me some simple words that changed my life. I discovered in later years that he'd been in the faculty lounge talking to some of the other teachers, all of whom were wondering if there was any hope for me.

"Listen, Callaway," he said, "your math marks aren't adding up. Your gift at science has yet to be discovered. Biology? Chemistry? Physics? Well, the experiments are not working."

I'd been told this before. It was not news to me.

But what he said next was the best news I'd heard in a long time: "I want you in my communication arts class. I think God has given you a gift in the area of communication."

For the first time in world history, a teacher wanted me in his class.

The very next day I had no trouble getting out of bed. I may have even combed my hair. I worked eagerly on my very first assignment: writing a poem for a poetry contest. I can't remember a single word I wrote, but I'll never forget Mr. Bienert standing at the front of the classroom, pulling five bucks from his wallet, and calling me forward.

"Congratulations, Callaway. You've got first prize," he said, stuffing the bill into my eager hand. "I want you to read this in chapel tomorrow. It's good stuff."

The next day my knees knocked and my hands shook as I walked to the podium. But I read that poem loudly before the entire school. All because someone thought I was talented enough to do it.

Through the years I've been influenced by many people. Some have scolded me, some have hollered at me, some have spanked me, and most have forgotten my birthday. But those who influenced me the most were not those who pointed out all my faults, but those who knew that God was bigger than my shortcomings. Those who influenced me the most didn't just point a finger; they pointed me heavenward and held out a helping hand.

None of us knows what God will do when we encourage someone. I almost flunked French class in high school. But now publishers are translating my writings into dozens of languages like Polish, Spanish, Chinese, English, and—you guessed it—French. I was born with a face for radio, but a video series of mine has been viewed in 80,000 churches around the world.

This is no tribute to me. It is a tribute to the goodness and greatness of a holy and loving God. And it's a tribute to people like Mr. Bienert, who believed in God enough to believe in me.

We may forget some birthdays. But let's not forget to encourage someone. Today.

Jesus wants us to see that the neighbor next door or the people sitting next to us on a plane or in a classroom are not interruptions to our schedule. They are there by divine appointment. Jesus wants us to see their needs, their loneliness, their longings, and He wants to give us the courage to reach out to them.

Rebecca Manley Pippert

35

Walk with Me

Someone has said that believers in Jesus and nonbelievers have something in common. We're both uptight about evangelism. That's me—uptight. I have to admit that most of the people in my life are Christians. Too often I'm too busy or too uptight to interact with people who do not share my view of the world. But lately I'm beginning to understand that I don't have to be Billy Graham to have an impact. I don't have to be Lee Strobel to have an answer. In fact, it's okay to be myself.

On a long flight to Dallas recently, I found myself seated beside a psychologist. Within five minutes of takeoff he had correctly diagnosed me as a Christian. "I've had lots of bad experiences with Christians," he confided.

"Really?" I said, rather excitedly. "Me too."

He laughed at my response and soon began talking about his work. "I counsel people with a rare disease. I'm sure you haven't heard of it," he said. "It's called Huntington's." This was probably the biggest surprise I ever want to experience on an airplane.

"Huntington's? Oh boy," I said, "That's…well, that's pretty close to home." For the next four hours we discussed the role Huntington's had played on my journey into trust. We talked about airline omelets and the Bible. We spoke of our favorite sports teams and the human condition.

"I grew up in the church, and I've been turned off by religion," he said, pouring himself another drink.

"Me too," I answered. "I tried it for a while, but it's a lousy substitute for a relationship with Jesus." He turned my way. "This may sound crazy to a psychologist, but I'm not sure where I'd be today if I didn't live in constant communication with someone I can't even see."

He smiled and shook his head slowly. "No," he said. "In my experience, it's not crazy at all."

When we parted ways, he kept shaking his head. "You've given me a few things to think about," he told me. I assured him that he had done the same for me.

Sometimes I wish I had more answers. Sometimes I wish I had more charisma. But I'm beginning to understand that what people need more than either of these is reality—the reality of a relationship that affects the way we respond to everything around us.

I've had the pleasure on several occasions of spending time with Joni Eareckson Tada, who has spent 40 years in a wheelchair following a diving accident. She told me, "Nothing will convince and convict those around us like the peaceful and positive way we respond to our hurts and distress. The unbelieving world—your neighbors, the guy at the gas station, the postman, the lady at the cleaners, your boss at work—is observing the way we undergo our trials." And, I might add, the way we respond to the trials of others.

A few years ago, a simple story had a profound impact on me. It was about two neighbors who were as different as day and night in the way they looked at the world. One was a lifelong Democrat, the other a Republican. One was a solid Christ-follower; the other wouldn't darken a church door if it was the only solid structure in a tornado. But for some reason they got along. They knew that discussing business or politics or faith was a surefire formula for disaster, so they stuck with talking about their marriages, their kids, and the yard work. When the nonbeliever's wife was diagnosed with a virulent form of cancer and died in three short months, his believing neighbor stepped in.

Recalling the night of his wife's death, the husband wrote, "I was in total despair. I went through the funeral preparations and the service like I was in a trance. And that night after the service, I just wanted to be alone. I left and went to the path along the river in our town and walked all night. But I did not walk alone. My neighbor, afraid for me, I suppose, stayed with me all night. He did not speak; he did not try and get me to go home; he did not even walk beside me. He just followed me. When the sun finally came up over the river the next morning, he came up to me and said, 'Let's get some breakfast.'

"I go to church now—my neighbor's church. I do not really like the pastor's politics sometimes. But a faith that can produce the kind of caring and love my neighbor showed me is something I want to be involved in. I want to be like that. I want to love and be loved like that the rest of my life."[2]

We may not have all the answers, but each of us is capable of this much. In a world characterized by loneliness and despair, we can reach out in love to those around us. Or, as St. Francis once said, "Preach the gospel all the time. If necessary, use words."

Looking back, I have to admit that most of my attempts to tell others about Jesus have seemed like a failure. What I fail to realize is that God is more than capable of making up for my inadequacies. This has rarely been clearer to me than on the cold winter night in Hamilton, Ontario, when I met Michael.

Moses wasn't qualified to lead God's people out of Egypt. He spoke with a stutter. He was reluctant and unwilling and he couldn't control his temper...In a very real sense not one of us is qualified, but it seems that God continually chooses the most unqualified to do His work, to bear His glory. If we are qualified, we tend to think that we have done the job ourselves. If we are forced to accept our evident lack of qualification, then there's no danger that we will confuse God's work with our own, or God's glory with our own.

Madeleine L'Engle

36

Two Things Last Forever

At the age of 26, Michael Slade is a neo-Nazi skinhead who enjoys reading the works of Aldous Huxley and Adolf Hitler. If you saw the two of us together, you might take a second look. Then a third. In his place of employment, Michael is paid to be irritable. In fact, the more irritable he gets, the better his results. Michael is a bill collector. Over the phone he intimidates people, and in the evenings he relies on alcohol and drugs to take the edge off. Most weekends he moves in with a 38-year-old divorcee and her two small children.

A neighbor invited Michael to a Saturday night meeting where I was speaking, and for some reason he came along. Afterward, Michael wandered over to where I was standing. With one hand he fingered a cigarette pack; with the other he thumbed through one of my books. When he bought it, I wrote in the front: "To Michael, Philippians 1:9-10." You may remember the verses: "And this is my prayer: that your love may abound more and more in knowledge and depth of insight, so that you may be able to discern what is best and may be pure and blameless until the day of Christ."

"Do you have a Bible?" I asked.

"Yeah, but I haven't read it yet."

"When you get home tonight, will you read these verses?"

He said he would. Then he was gone.

The next day on the flight home I prayed for Michael. I knew I would never see him again, but for some reason I couldn't get him off my mind. Perhaps it was the frustration I felt from knowing I hadn't said the right thing or given him the right verses. I was too busy selling books.

That night I fell asleep praying for Michael.

The following Wednesday the phone rang. You guessed it. Bill collectors can track you down anywhere, and I was glad he had. "I read your book through without stopping," he began. "I laughed, I cried, and I…I just had to talk to you." On Saturday after the meeting, Michael went home, found the Bible under a bottle of Jack Daniel's, and somehow located Philippians. He started to read it and couldn't stop. "I told my girlfriend we've been doing some stuff we shouldn't be doin,'" he said.

Sunday night Michael couldn't sleep. He paced the floor. "Then, I heard my name called out loud. Twice. I woke up my roommate, but it wasn't him." All that week Michael had trouble thinking of anything else.

As we talked, Michael gave me a firsthand account of one who spent his life desperately seeking pleasure, only to come up empty. "I've made a mess of my life," he said. "If I, like, come to God, will he make me comfortable?"

I paused for a moment. "No," I said, "God won't make you

comfortable." I tried to recite C.S. Lewis' words: "I didn't go to religion to make me happy. I always knew a bottle of port would do that. If you want a religion to make you feel really comfortable, I certainly don't recommend Christianity."

Lewis went on to say, "The Christian religion does not begin in comfort; it begins in dismay...comfort is the one thing you cannot get by looking for it. If you look for truth, you may find comfort in the end: If you look for comfort you will not get either comfort or truth—only wishful thinking...and, in the end, despair."

Michael was silent for a minute. I told him how difficult the last few years of my life had been. I said God had not taken our problems away, but he had sent his Holy Spirit, the Comforter, to help us carry them. I told him about Jesus' death on the cross, the end of a life that could not be described as comfortable. I talked about the Bible's account of his resurrection and the hope it had brought to my life.

Again, Michael was silent.

Before we hung up I tried to show him how to find the gospel of John. It wasn't easy. Finally I said, "Read right through it and ask yourself this question: Who is Jesus?"

That night I went to sleep praying for Michael. This time I was sure I wouldn't hear back. My words had faltered. I hadn't always said what I meant. And what I had said was anything but popular. People don't get all excited about things like crucifixion, lack of comfort, carrying crosses, and repenting of sin. But once again I underestimated the power of God's Word.

Sunday night Michael called again. This time we talked about his job, about his girlfriend, and about sex, drugs, and rock 'n' roll. But mostly we talked about Jesus. Then we prayed together, and Michael asked Christ to be the biggest part of his life.

We were 2000 miles apart but closer than we'd ever been before.

When I wrote my first book, I told God that the midnights alone in front of the computer would be well worth it if just one person was in heaven as a result. He heard my prayer that Sunday night. He delights in doing that—through me, through you, and through all who realize that this world and everything in it will one day pass away, but two things will last forever: God's Word and people.

The richest life you'll ever live will be invested in these. Just ask our next guest, Carl Medearis.

If we are devoted to the cause of humanity, we shall soon be crushed and broken-hearted, for we shall often meet with more ingratitude from men than we would from a dog; but if our motive is love to God, no ingratitude can hinder us from serving our fellow men.

OSWALD CHAMBERS

37

Friend of Muslims

One of the surest ways to avoid a rich life is to embrace paranoia and fear. You may want to start with a steady diet of the evening news. Tonight on CNN I learned that a pandemic is about to sweep the globe and that football stadiums are dangerous places. I also met a guy who got rabies from his own dog. After half an hour of quiet music, my blood pressure had nearly normalized, but still I found myself wondering what possible good it could do me to know 86 percent of what CNN spent the last week talking about.

Few occupations excel at bottling paranoia and selling it more effectively than the media. In the past decade they warned us of disaster after disaster to come. They were wrong. The only true disasters that arrived were those they hadn't warned us of.

It helps to remind ourselves that Those in the Know have consistently misdiagnosed the future, dispensing tablets of fear and ridiculous notions of what we should do in the face of it. Somehow we survived the Y2K hoax (with basements full of canned goods), at least three global pandemics, and online viruses that "threaten to destroy the personal computer, the Internet, and possibly your life."

In some of my most vibrant childhood memories, I am crouching under a maple school desk, my hands clasped over my head, staving off nuclear invasion while crossing my eyes at a pretty little girl whose name I can't recall.

In June 1974, *Time* magazine ran a cover story called "The New Ice Age." Today anyone not embracing the opposite belief is placed in the same cell as the flat-earth theorists. Now, I'm not dim-bulbed enough to deny that climate change happens or recommend that we go on pulling SUVs behind our motor homes while smoking plastic bags, but I sometimes wonder if we should allow people who cannot predict the weather for Thursday to tell us how warm it will be in 30 years.[3]

I ask people how they are doing and they say, "Awesome." But I can tell that what they really are is scared.

One told me to watch a YouTube video about how Muslims are taking over the earth. I watched it and immediately became paranoid. After all, according to the video, the average North American couple is having one and a half children. The average Muslim family is having eight. In 40 years, five out of every three people you meet will be a Muslim.

I didn't know what to do with this fear until I decided to mention my concern to my friend Carl Medearis. Carl has spent the last 25 years in the Arab world teaching Muslim university students, business professionals, and political leaders to live by the principles of Jesus.

Twenty-five years ago he and his wife and children sold everything and moved to Beirut (and you thought I was crazy). "We didn't know anyone," recalls Carl, "didn't speak Arabic, and didn't really know what we were going to do." The country was a mess. It was bombed-out and burned up, and he believed he had the answer. So rather than embrace fear, Carl embraced the people. He began teaching English and Western history, learning Arabic, making friends, and having meals with them.

"So Carl," I asked him, "should I panic?"

"Why?"

"The Muslims are coming. They're taking over."

"Well, last time I checked," said Carl, "God was still in control."

"Yeah, but…um—"

"Listen, in places like Sudan, Iran, and Iraq, people are coming to faith in Jesus. That includes hundreds of thousands of Iranian Shiite Muslims—the majority because of personal spiritual revelation and through miracles. Many times I have had Muslims tell me, 'I had a dream about Jesus last night,' and then I 'happened' to stumble across their path, and they're open to receive what I have to say."

"So you think maybe Jesus has things figured out?"

"In a hotel in Basra, Iraq, I found myself talking with three employees. One said that 20 years earlier, someone told his father, 'Jesus has a book out and you should do whatever it takes to get one.' He asked me, 'Does Jesus have a book?' I said, 'Yes, and I have one in my room.' I almost tripped over the carpet going to get it, I was so excited. When I presented it to him, he held it to his forehead, kissed it, broke down in tears, and ran out of the hotel. Later he came running back to tell us that his father said it was the real book of Jesus. 'Do you have more?' he asked. 'We want to give it to our relatives.' God is at work, Phil."

"What does a Muslim think of when he hears the word *Jesus?*"

"There's immediate respect," Carl quickly answered. "They may not believe that he is the Son of God, but the Qur'an mentions Jesus about 90 times, all of them positive. He's called the Word of God, the Messiah—although they don't really understand what that means. He did miracles, lived a pure and sinless life, was born of a virgin, ascended to heaven, and will come back at the end to judge the living and the dead. If a Muslim says to me, 'I believe in Jesus; he's a great prophet,' instead of saying, 'Yeah, but…' I say, 'That's fantastic. Let's talk about him.'"

"I guess what I know about Islam, I've learned from the news."

"Listen. I have lived and loved and shared and grieved with Muslims for more than twenty-five years. In the few acts of violence I have encountered, I have never once seen a radical terrorist living in accordance with any higher standard of values: Muslim, Christian, or otherwise. The great majority of Muslims want safe and peaceful lives with their families and friends."

"But I've had Christians tell me that there are no bridge-building opportunities within Islam."

"They're dead wrong. The Qur'an is packed full of stuff about Jesus. So when I begin a conversation with a Muslim, I start with Jesus. I start in the Gospels, and when they need to know why the crucifixion had to happen, I go to the Old Testament and then the writings of Paul—actually, the rest of the whole Bible explains the life, death, resurrection, and ministry of Jesus. But I start with Jesus, and Muslims don't just put up with it—they love it. Every year they celebrate *Eid al-Adha,* a festival where they slaughter a sheep for the atonement of their sins because Abraham was asked to sacrifice his son. God provided a lamb that takes away the sins of the world. Does that sound like a bridge or what?"

"So how should I treat my Muslim neighbor?"

"First of all, have fun. Laughter and hanging out over food and friends anywhere in the world opens people's hearts. If you don't know how to party, get help from someone who does. At the same time, know and understand the cultural norms so you don't offend more people than you win. If you're celebrating with Muslims, it will be a clean party. There's a lot of talk, friendship, and lots of laughs."

"What else?"

"I start with what we agree on. We agree that Jesus of Nazareth lived. So let's talk about his life and decide who he was. I tell them, 'I don't want to be following the wrong Jesus. There may be things I don't know about him, and hopefully you can point this out to me and we'll grow closer to him together.' I have yet to find anyone anywhere who's not ready to do that. You and I know that Jesus is Lord and Savior, that he is God in the flesh, but if someone we're talking to doesn't know that, it is presumptuous to begin there. I don't argue with my Muslim friends. I try to nudge the discussion back to the person, works, and words of Jesus. We are not here to convert people to Christianity, but to turn people's hearts toward the Creator."

"So your success in leading Muslims to Jesus didn't come because you panicked?"

"I just hang out with people, try to make friends, and talk about Jesus all the time. I don't build friendships in order to share the gospel. I just build friendships because I love people, and I share Jesus because he's the most important thing in my life. I've said to Muslims, 'You talk about Jesus, and he's in the Qur'an, but I don't see much action. What if we together really thought about following him?' I've said this in Saudi Arabia in public places. I've said it to Saudi royal family members, and they never say, 'No, you can't do that.' Muslims are not offended by this message. When I meet someone, I don't start with differences; I honor the culture and try to fit in. When most people talk about faith, they tend to get very quickly into things that we disagree on. Jesus didn't do that."

Some turn to Larry King, but I find that talking to Carl is like opening a window on a stuffy day.[4] None of us knows what lies ahead, but we can know who will be there waiting for us when we get there.

"We serve a risen Jesus," says Carl. "There's enough fear going around these days—finances, terrorism, and stuff like that. We need to constantly bring it back to him. People love sensationalism, and what makes the news are the negative stories, not 'Muslims are nicer than you think.' But I think it's the message the church in the West needs to hear, and I believe it reflects the message of Jesus."

Regard your good name as the richest jewel you can possibly be possessed of...The way to gain a good reputation is to endeavor to be what you desire to appear.

SOCRATES

38

What About Barb?

One of the finest perks of being an author is the chance to meet children who look up at you with wide eyes and ask you to sign a book. Or sometimes they say, "Did you really write *Green Eggs and Ham?*" During the last ten years, however, it has become increasingly problematic for me to inscribe their names correctly in my books. One little girl asked me to do so and told me her name: Gerdy Bell. Or at least that's what I thought she said. I asked her to spell it. She said, "Kiertzibelle. K-i-e-r-t-z-i-b-e-l-l-e." She spelled it quickly, causing me to think that she'd had a little practice at it.

Now, I'm old enough to remember the days when there were approximately six options for names. Parents chose from a short list of single-syllable monikers that had been approved by the Federal Name Police, an organization founded because folk singers were experimenting with banned substances and naming their children Star, Moon Unit, and Whoops.

In those days, available names included Don, John, Tom, Bob, and Phil. If your child was a girl, a slight variation would suffice: Dawn, Jenn, Tammy, Bobbi, or Phyllis. Not anymore. Today parents are making up names in the delivery room. "Hi, my name is Dawn, and this is my daughter, *HAAAAALP!*"

Each of the following is a registered name. I kid you not.

Abishag Lettuce
Peaches Honeyblossom
Frou-frou
Fifi
Trixibelle
Feather

In Britain, there are children named Reebok, Adidas, and Superman. There are 6 Gandalphs, 39 Gazzas, 36 Arsenals, and almost 2000 boys named Tiger.

U.S. federal census records indicate that parents have recently bestowed the following names on their children: Fanny Pack, Post Office, Warren Peace, Nice Carr, Garage Empty, King Arthur, Helen Troy, Candy Stohr, Mary Christmas, Rasp Berry, Happy Day, Ima Pigg, Ima Muskrat, and Ima Nut.[5]

And those are the ones fit for print.

Remember the names we thought Bart Simpson was making up for prank calls? The infamous Al Caholic, Anita Bath, and Amanda Hugginkiss? They are on the list too.

Strange names are nothing new. But people used to hide them behind initials. The parents of C.S. Lewis thought Clive Staples had a nice ring to it. Clive did not. A fine young man I grew up with was known as T.J. Thompson. We just called him T.J. I never thought to ask what it stood for, so imagine my surprise when I discovered years later that it stood for Thaddeus Josephus. It's a good thing we didn't know this in fourth grade because we may have beat him up twice a week.

In our town, there's a dog named Viggo. I met him and his owner one night when I was out walking our dog Mojo.[6] The dogs liked each other immediately and engaged in dog-type behavior while Viggo's owner and I talked. "I named the dog after the movie star Viggo

Mortensen," she told me. I wonder what Viggo would think of having a wiener dog as his namesake.

Though the dogs won't be suing us anytime soon, the children are. A growing list of lawsuits has been launched against parents citing something called "name abuse." A Swedish couple refused to legally name their newborn son (in protest of Sweden's naming law). They were threatened with a fine of about $600, so they submitted the name Brfxxccxxmnpcccclllmmnprxvclmnckssqlbb11116 (pronounced *albin*). The Swedish court rejected the name. The couple tried to change the spelling of the name to *A* (also pronounced *albin*), but the court rejected that as well. The boy's name was eventually agreed upon as Albin Gustaf Tarzan Hallin.

I wish I were making this up.

Naming Names

Here are a few suggestions on naming children:

- Avoid names that will draw curious crowds and media exposure, spawn websites, or cause ripples of laughter in classrooms and gymnasiums.
- Avoid names your child will have to spell for everyone she meets.
- Picture yourself standing on the front steps at night yelling the name. How will "Please Cope," or "Justin Case" (both real names) sound? Will neighbors call the police on you?

Proverbs 22:1 tells us that a good name is to be chosen over great riches, that "to be esteemed is better than silver or gold."

Far more important than the names we give our children is the reputation they will carry with them through life. They will need to build that reputation themselves, of course, but we have much to do with getting them started down the right road.

For me, one of the most heartbreaking aspects of traveling the country is hearing the stories of those who have been abused, belittled, ridiculed, and scarred by selfish, shortsighted and sinful parents. Truly rich people are aware that their choices will echo through the coming generations, that what they do and say matters well past today.

Early on the morning of April 15, 1865, the well-known actor John Wilkes Booth and a friend stopped at the Maryland home of Dr. Samuel Alexander Mudd. Clearly in pain, Booth asked the doctor to treat his broken leg. So began a long-lasting controversy as to whether Dr. Mudd knew that Booth had assassinated President Abraham Lincoln and failed to surrender him to military authorities. In recent years, a U.S. congressman introduced the "Samuel Mudd Relief Act," hoping to exonerate the doctor. But guilty or not, even today, when we speak of someone with a bad name we say, "His name is Mudd." When people hear your name, what will they think of? How will you be remembered?

Proverbs 3:3-6 offers us the key to passing on the legacy of a name worth remembering:

> Let love and faithfulness never leave you;
> bind them around your neck,
> write them on the tablet of your heart.
>
> Then you will win favor and a good name
> in the sight of God and man.

Beauty fades, but to be married to someone who makes you laugh every day—ah, that's a real treat.

Joanne Woodward, married to the late actor Paul Newman for 50 years

39

The Power of Commitment

The great philosopher Socrates once wrote, "By all means, marry. If you get a good wife, you will become very happy. If you get a bad one, you'll become a philosopher."

I'm no philosopher, but I believe that one of the most valuable heirlooms my parents left me is their platinum marriage. I once asked Dad about the secret to it, and without hesitation he said, "Senility. I wake up each morning and I can't remember who this old girl is. So each day is a new adventure." When Mom finally quit elbowing him, he got serious.

"One word," he said, squeezing her hand. "Commitment."

You don't have to spend much time in the supermarket checkout line to know that commitment is hardly a hallmark of our culture—or of Hollywood. Robin Givens married her tennis instructor—for one day. The eighth of Zsa Zsa Gabor's nine marriages also lasted one day. And Carmen Electra and Dennis Rodman stuck it out a whopping nine days. Among the most married stars are these:

John Huston (six times)

Rex Harrison (six times)

Stan Laurel (seven times)

Liz Taylor (eight times)

Mickey Rooney (eight times)

Standing in a grocery store near the chocolate bars, I picked out a tabloid and read of Rex and Teresa LeGalley, a young couple who wanted to ensure that their marriage would stand the test of time. After all, it was Teresa's second and Rex's third. So they drew up a 16-page prenuptial agreement with such explicit directives as "nothing will be left on the floor overnight—unless packing for a trip," what time they'll go to bed, how often they'll have sex, which gasoline they'll purchase, and who will do the laundry. Said Teresa, "This is the plan that we think will keep us married for 50 or 60 years."

When I told this to Dad, he had another one-word response: "Ha!"

Separate Vacations

Occasionally Hollywood surprises us with good news.

Famed singer and actress Bette Midler, who has been married since 1984 to artist Martin von Haselberg, was asked about the key to their marriage. Midler responded, "Separate vacations." Then, like my dad, she got serious. "We're committed," she said. "We're in it for the long haul. Besides, you really don't get to know a person until you've known them a long time, and we don't know each other yet. Sometimes it's been a struggle, but amazingly, we didn't give up."

Prolific author Stephen King had a simple answer when asked how he has stayed productive for so long: "I stayed healthy and stayed married."

When asked by *US* magazine about the secret to his 53-year marriage, James Garner, the star of *Maverick* and *The Rockford Files,* said, "Consideration. You have to care for [your spouse] and do a lot of forgiving and forgetting. It's a two-way street. A lot of people don't get married because they know they can get out of it any minute. Hey, it was difficult for me to make that commitment, but when I make them, I stick with them."

I remember reading of an elderly couple whose family had thrown a golden anniversary party for them. The husband was deeply touched by their kindness and stood to thank them. Then he looked at his wife of fifty years and tried to put into words just how he felt about her. Lifting his glass he said, "My dear wife, after fifty years I've found you tried and true." Everyone smiled their approval, but not his wife. She had hearing trouble, so she cupped one hand behind an ear and said, "Eh?" (She must have been a Canadian.)

Her husband repeated himself loudly, "AFTER FIFTY YEARS I'VE FOUND YOU TRIED AND TRUE!"

His wife shot back, "Well, let me tell YOU something—after fifty years I'm tired of you too!"

Thankfully, commitment doesn't need to be like that. Marriage is not a life sentence, it is a joyful privilege. Paul Brand, the missionary doctor who worked for many years among leprosy victims in India, said these challenging words: "As I enter my sixth decade of marriage I can say without a flicker of hesitation that the basic human virtue of faithfulness to one partner is the most joyful way of life...I have always trusted my wife completely, and she me. We have each been able to channel love and commitment and intimacy to one person—a lifelong investment that is now, in old age, paying rich dividends."

A friend once told me that his parents always got along, that he had never heard them disagree and had certainly never heard them argue. I finally stopped laughing long enough to tell him that I couldn't say that about my parents. But I never doubted their commitment to each other. What kept my parents committed? "Simple obedience to God," said Mom, who always gave more serious answers than Dad. "We put him first, and he helped us love each other."

I Can't Love Without You

When I was a boy I often caught Mom and Dad praying or reading the Bible together. Mom was a tenacious Presbyterian who didn't mind preaching to me every chance she got. "Unless the LORD builds the house, its builders labor in vain," she said.[7] I have kept a note of hers to this day. It reads, "Only with Christ at the center of our marriage, at the center of our home, at the center of everything we do, can we experience the greatest joy and fulfillment possible."

My wife and I have made a commitment to read the Bible and pray together before we go to sleep each night. We haven't always achieved that goal. But when we follow through on this simple commitment, it makes a world of difference in our marriage. For one thing, I find it very difficult to read certain things aloud to my wife without it having a dramatic effect on the way I treat her. I bump into verses like this: "Clothe yourselves with compassion, kindness, humility, gentleness and patience. Bear with each other and forgive whatever grievances you may have against one another. Forgive as the Lord forgave you. And over all these virtues put on love, which binds them all together in perfect unity" (Colossians 3:12-14).

Christ alone gives us the power to love others in this way.

I am well aware of my many friends who will read these words and feel they have failed. Thank God he helps us learn from the past and find strength for today and bright hope for tomorrow. Thank God that he delights in helping us stand up and start again.

A few months before his death at the age of 87, Gregory Peck, the famous movie star, was asked, "What would you like to leave behind?" He didn't mention his movie legacy, his money, or his mansion. He didn't talk about the regrets from his failed first marriage, though I'm sure he had some. Peck said, "I want to be remembered as a good husband and father. I want to be remembered by my wife as someone who made her happy." They were married 48 years. Wrote one biographer, "Scandal never touched him."

Despite our failures and shortcomings, all of us would like to be remembered that way, wouldn't we? And regardless of where we've been, we can start today.

It may not be the deepest thing you'll ever read, but I'd rather be a happily married man than a philosopher. Any day.

No man has a good enough memory to make a successful liar.

Abraham Lincoln

40

The Stuff We Leave Behind

Well, I finally did it. After years of checking out prices, I talked myself into buying one. After years of admiring those tiny leaves and gnarled branches, I mustered up the courage to bring one home. It sits in my living room window now, soaking up the sun's rays, reaching out for moisture, and growing…ever so slowly.

I didn't even know they existed until I watched *The Karate Kid*. The wise old master pruned and wired and clipped away, and then one day he presented a lonely and mistreated boy with an ancient tree ten inches tall. The tree spoke to the boy of endurance, of perseverance, of growth—things he would need to bring the movie to a happy end. Since then, I've wanted a bonsai tree for myself. But they looked too much like work (all that wiring and clipping). They also looked too much like money (some were as much as $1000).

I had no idea how crazy people get about these things. They give the trees names and have bonsai conventions. They pay $200 a month just to board them at nurseries where they are fed and tended by professionals (the trees, that is). Daizo Iwasaki, chairman and chief executive of Nangoku Sangyo, has collected 30,000 specimens. He employs 15 people just to care for them. In Japan it is considered bad form to talk openly of the price of these trees, but with a little extra sleuthing I was able to discover that a 250-year-old juniper recently sold for $2 million.

Thankfully I found a small one for only $16, and it made no sense to leave it in the store.

The trouble with me purchasing a bonsai, however, is not only the cost but also the fact that I was born with a black thumb. In fact, if you have a plant you don't like, give it to me. I don't know what it is. I water and weed with the best of them, but plants see me coming and they change color. I walk by and they wilt. Things will be different with this tree though. Some nights, after the kids are tucked in, you'll find me with the perfect pruning instrument (my wife's fingernail clippers), lovingly snipping, trimming, and wiring until it's all I can see when I close my eyes.

If the lady who sold me this tree is right, a well-cared for bonsai should last a few hundred years. "Even longer than me," I told her. So I'll keep snipping, trimming, and wiring, and perhaps this tree will be around long after I've hung up the fingernail clippers.

Of course, I'd like to leave behind a little more than a gnarled old tree, but after a story I heard this morning, I'm wondering what could be more important.

Last summer, an acquaintance of mine took his 12-year-old son on a weekend fishing trip. The purpose was to teach the boy the facts of life, to let him know the wonderful joys of married love. "Sex is a gift from God to be celebrated and saved for the one you marry," he told his son, as they stood waist-deep in a crystal clear stream, casting flies after rainbow trout.

The boy had no reason to doubt him—until a month later, when his dad walked out the front door with the same suitcase he'd taken along on that fishing trip. He left behind a devastated family. He left behind the awful truth: For over a year he'd been having an affair with a married woman. His boy may never be the same.

Since I heard the news, I've been thinking about the stuff we leave behind. Whether we like it or not, the impact we make is almost always determined not by the words we say, but by the life we live. Those who impact us most are not those who preach to us, but those who live their lives quietly, gracefully, and faithfully, like the stars in the heavens.

Later this week, I'll go back to that store and buy three more bonsai trees—one for each of the kids.

Perhaps years from now in some far-off place, they'll be able to look at a bonsai basking in their living room window and think of their dad. Long after my words have stopped ringing in their ears, they'll have a small reminder of the stuff that mattered to me.

I pray that the tree will speak to them of character. Of perseverance. Of faithfulness.

I hope it will remind them that although their dad had his share of twists and bends, he grew strong and faithful under the loving hand of the Master.

Part Six

Rich People Have the Last Laugh

Within the space of two months, a friend of mine lost both of his teenage sons, David and Michael, to muscular dystrophy. Not long before David died, a schoolmate agreed to push him through a mall one Saturday. It was the Christmas season. Surrounded by frenzied shoppers, his friend stopped the wheelchair, bent down and asked a question: "If you could have just one wish, what would it be?" Trapped in a wheelchair, unable to move his arms and legs, David replied, "Nothing. I've got Jesus. My mom and dad love me. And I've got friends like you to help me over the speed bumps."

Then, smiling an awkward smile his friends and family had come to love, he added quietly, "Besides, I know where I'm going. And there ain't no wheelchairs there."

I've met millionaires and billionaires. I've talked to CEOs and VIPs. But I've never met anyone richer than David. Strapped in a wheelchair—with no wishes, but filled with hope.

Here are a few stories of what it takes to finish well.

The truly rich find no lasting pleasure in that which fades away, but in bringing purpose and hope to others, in setting their sights on eternity.

You gave me everything to live with
and nothing to live for.

A teenager's suicide note to his parents

41

Good News for Weary Travelers

On a train trip years ago, Mark Twain found himself seated next to someone with the gift of gloom. The fellow traveler, reflecting on all that was wrong with the world, said to Twain, "Do you realize that every time I take a breath, 10,000 people on this planet die?"

Mark Twain thought for a minute and then replied, "Hmm... ever try cloves?"

Have you ever sat beside such a person? I did the other day. We were over Colorado, cruising at 31,000 feet, and he kept bringing me down to earth. Life as a government employee was giving him more than his share of ulcers, and to complicate matters, he suffered from a serious paralysis of the funny bone. Flipping through a magazine, he showed me some appalling statistics. Frowning through a Diet Coke, he told me of the moral chaos. "Things are bad all over," he said as a young child with a "No Fear" ball cap tried unsuccessfully to play peekaboo with him. "I give the world five years before the next big bang. Maybe six. You just watch."

Although I'm normally a mild-mannered sort (even more so when I've swallowed a motion sickness pill), I thought I'd better say something. "Yes, the times are bad," I told him, "but they're the only times we have. If the big bang comes, I hope it finds me doing something productive, like dating my wife or playing catch with my kids or maybe planting a tree." I'd read something like that in a book once, and I thought it sounded wise.

He didn't say anything, so in lieu of cloves, I offered him a stick of gum and then sat quietly, thinking about his comments. I couldn't argue with him. I read the news and watch the television.

In fact, the previous night in my hotel room, the film *City Slickers* was showing. In the film, comedian Billy Crystal plays the part of a bored salesman who is invited to his son's school to tell the children about his work. When Crystal launches into a deadpan monologue, he leaves the kids bewildered but the rest of us smiling.

> Value this time in your life, kids, because this is the time in your life when you still have your choices. It goes by so fast.
>
> When you're a teenager, you think you can do anything, and you do. Your twenties are a blur. Thirties, you raise your family, you make a little money, and you think to yourself, "What happened to my twenties?"
>
> Forties, you grow a little pot belly, you grow another chin. The music starts to get too loud, one of your old girlfriends from high school becomes a grandmother.
>
> Fifties, you have a minor surgery—you'll call it a procedure, but it's a surgery.
>
> Sixties, you'll have a major surgery, the music is still loud, but it doesn't matter because you can't hear it anyway.
>
> Seventies, you and the wife retire to Fort Lauderdale. You start eating dinner at 2:00 in the afternoon, you have lunch around 10:00, breakfast the night before, spend most of your time wandering around malls looking for the ultimate soft yogurt and muttering, "How come the kids don't call? How come the kids don't call?"
>
> The eighties, you'll have a major stroke, and you end up babbling with some Jamaican nurse who your wife can't stand but who you call "Mama."
>
> Any questions?

What a vivid picture of an empty life, a life without meaning or purpose. A life that seems to shout, "Hey, why go on? Where's the hope?"

One night I watched as Mike Tyson, retired boxer and former international celebrity, seemed to shout this question in a television interview. Sitting alone on a white leather couch, he spoke openly of the hopelessness of his life. With marble staircases rising behind him and diamond-studded rings adorning his hands, he talked of his boredom. Behind him, ornate columns rose from a tranquil pool, and everywhere there were signs that since earning as much as $30 million for one fight, he had denied himself no pleasure. Built on 17 acres, his 61-room estate was the largest house in Connecticut. It boasted 38 baths, 7 kitchens, a disco, a gym, and a master bedroom with five television sets. It was one of four mansions the disgraced boxing legend owned around the world.

Yet for Tyson life was meaningless.

When he confessed this to the interviewer, his words were met with a bewildered stare. "You have all this and you feel that way...?" asked the reporter, raising both eyebrows.

"Yeah," said Tyson. "I stayed here probably four times...I guess I am extremely bored."

In another honest interview, pop star Boy George admitted the truth:

> Growing up, you dream of being liked and being successful. You imagine that fame can fill your needs. You just think, let me scale that pinnacle. But nothing outside yourself can make you feel whole. Not fame, not sex, not drugs, not money. None of those things work. Nothing can fill you up. And believe me, 'cause I've tried them all. In some ways, I am the modern Elvis.

Like Mike Tyson, Leo Tolstoy achieved worldwide acclaim. Like Boy George, he had searched everywhere for meaning, only to come up empty. But then the Russian author of *War and Peace* made a simple discovery that changed everything:

> I began to draw near to the believers among the poor, simple, and ignorant, the pilgrims, monks, and peasants. The more I contemplated the lives of these simple folk, the more deeply was I convinced of the reality of their faith...for it alone gave life a meaning and made it worth living...I felt that I had only truly lived when I believed in God. God is life. Live to seek God, and life will not be without him. The light that then shone never left me...I came to know that God is all we need.

I must confess that there are days when I feel like my fellow traveler. After all, you don't have to be a government employee to see that the outlook is not so good. But then I'm reminded that in the darkest of times, hope can shine the brightest.

Is hope a pie-in-the-sky illusion? Does it make us complacent, content to leave the world as it is?

I used to think so, but then I sat down beside another traveler on the darkest voyage of all. A voyage that would change him—and me—forever.

Life is an onion. You peel it off one layer at a time, and sometimes you weep.

Carl Sandburg

42

Divine Mathematics

I stood looking out our front window at the morning rain and shaking my head. How could it be? My friend and mentor's only child. His teenage daughter. Gone. Days earlier, she had wrestled on the carpet with our kids. Two days ago, she was so full of life. But last night all that changed. Last night after church, she joined a carload of friends driving down the highway singing, "Soon and very soon, we are going to see the King..." Suddenly headlights burst in their faces, and two of them were ushered into the presence of the King.

My own daughter, Rachael, brought me back into the present, pulling at my sleeve now. "Why are you crying?"

"It's Janella, honey. She's with Jesus." The words seemed distant. Detached. Too implausible to be real.

"But if she's in heaven, why are you sad?"

"Ah, Rachael—"

The phone rang. It was Paul, the newly bereaved father. "The grief comes and goes in waves," he told me. "Right now I don't see how I can go on. What is there to live for?"

What could I say? My friend...always joyful, so quick to laugh, so ready to share a bear hug. But now, crying like a baby.

A year ago in this same kitchen, he had talked to me about living every moment as if it were our last. Picking up a banana, he had given it a swift karate chop and then cleaned up the mess while my wife stood by, shaking her head. That same day he ate a live cricket just to watch us squirm. "We did this in Haiti all the time," he said, speaking of his days as a missionary kid. "North American crickets aren't bad either. A little on the skinny side though." But today there was no laughter. Today we wept together and said very little.

Three months passed in a wilderness of pain and loneliness and deep depression. Then one day, Paul and his wife, Judy, heard a knock at the door. A representative from World Exchange Program who had heard of their loss had a question: Would they be interested in hosting a 17-year-old student from Luxembourg? "He's been waiting for two years," she pleaded. "Soon he'll be too old for the program. He's paid his money, and I want him in a Christian host family." Her enthusiasm seemed foreign to the emptiness in their hearts. "It's only a ten-month commitment."

Sitting at the kitchen table, they listened with growing sympathy for this 17-year-old orphan. His name was Yves. His mother had died when he was only 7; his father, when he was 14. Reviewing Yves' application, they noticed that he was allergic to dogs and cats. And they saw his comment on religion: "No interest. An atheist."

Against the advice of others to make no major decisions for a year, they found themselves at the airport one August evening, waiting with mixed emotions to welcome a stranger into their home.

The next morning, Yves accompanied his hosts to a predominantly black church, vibrant with enthusiasm. *What did I get myself into?* he wondered. *They're into some strange cult.*

Life at school was just as bewildering. Strange surroundings, strange people, strange language. Finally, Yves enrolled in a public-speaking class. His first assignment: Give a speech in front of his high-school peers. In the process of correcting Yves' grammar, Paul read of the boy's admiration for the way they were handling the loss of their daughter and his admission, "I'm beginning to think about God."

Neither Paul nor Judy knew much about raising boys, nor did they know that a year earlier, in the grip of depression, Yves had scribbled out a note: "God, if you're real, get me out of Luxembourg and find me a family."

One night while eating dessert together, Paul and Judy talked about Janella. "I picture her in heaven now, cheering us on," said Paul. As they talked, the conversation moved to Yves, and they were shocked to discover that both wanted to adopt him. And something deep inside them said it was the right thing to do.

And so, while the three did dishes together one evening, Paul popped the question. "Yves, how would you like to be adopted?" Smothering them in a soapy hug, Yves began to cry.

Judy took to mothering with enthusiasm, but Paul found himself struggling to give his new son a place in his heart. Painful reminders of Janella played havoc with his emotions, and he wanted to withdraw from Yves.

One dark winter morning at 1:30, they were roused from a pleasant sleep as their new son danced into the room. "Wake up! Wake up!" he shouted. "It's true—he came in!"

Though Paul and Judy hadn't pushed their faith on him, Yves had heard a clear message: Regardless of how dark the night, a relationship with Jesus Christ gives us hope for the future. He had knelt before God that very night and been adopted once again.

As winter turned to spring, Yves' younger brother, Mike, came for a visit. On the third day of Mike's visit, Paul asked the question the new family had discussed before Mike's arrival: "How would you like to join our family and be our second son?" His face registered amazement and confusion. In Luxembourg, an unrelated family never adopts a teenager, let alone two. He would think it over.

Later in the summer, Mike returned for a second visit. On the night before his return to Luxembourg, he embraced Judy and with tears streaming down his face said, "Congratulations, Mom." Then giving Paul a polite and reserved hug, he said, "Congratulations, Dad." The following January, he arrived to begin a new life.

February sunshine streamed through the kitchen window that Saturday morning, and Judy's homemade pancakes smothered in maple syrup beckoned from the table. Paul had just opened his mouth to ask the blessing, when Mike said, "Dad, can I pray?" Curiosity flashed across three faces. "Dear Lord," he began in a thick German accent, "tank you for da beautiful night, especially for me..." *What could be next?* they wondered. "I asked you into my heart and YOU CAME IN!" Pancakes were forgotten, and tears flowed again as they all jumped up to hug him.

By February, Mike's adoption was official. In less than a year, the Steinhauer family had doubled.

One Sunday morning, as the new family sat together listening to a sermon, Paul's pastor moved away from his pulpit, looked at them with a smile, and began talking of God's divine mathematics. "Only God could take one and add two!" he said.

How true, agrees Paul. "Only God could take a grief so wrenching you want to end it all and transform it into a joy that makes you want to start all over again. As for God, his way is perfect."

Has it been easy ever since? You better believe it hasn't. Yet Paul and Judy have told us that "whether God gives or takes away, his name is to be praised. He doesn't owe us any answers here, but one day we'll understand."

Some wonder if the hope of heaven causes one to live a life detached from the real world down here. Paul and Judy give testimony to the opposite. Those who do the most for this world are those who think most of the next.

Yves would agree. As he said one day in the kitchen, "When I get to heaven, two things I will do. First, see Jesus face-to-face. Then, find Janella and thank her for making room for me in this family."

When I was 40, my doctor advised me that a man in his forties shouldn't play tennis. I heeded his advice carefully and could hardly wait until I reached 50 to start again.

Hugo Black

43

Aging Grace

Let me ask you a question. It's been on my mind since a friend asked it during our biweekly gathering of the Circle of Six. If you haven't heard of us yet, allow me to explain that we are six handsome, middle-aged men who get together every other Tuesday to sample chocolate cheesecakes and consider deep questions, such as "I wonder if we should go on a diet?"

Of course we discuss other things too. Lately, for instance, we've been talking about the aging process. The discussion started with an interesting question. A question I'd like you to consider:

Do you look forward to growing old?

Of course, each of us in the Circle of Six had a different answer. Personally, I did my best to avoid the question as long as I could by stuffing my mouth full of cheesecake. *Age is relative,* I thought. Fifty is old when you're 15, but not when you're 90. Furthermore, aging is the one thing we can't do anything about. If we're alive, we're aging (some of us more swiftly than others). But when I ran out of cheesecake, I had to answer the question. Let me be rather honest: I've nursed parents through Alzheimer's and dementia, and I must admit, I don't look forward to growing old.

I'm not alone on this one. Watching *20/20,* I learned about a

European woman who spent her $100,000 inheritance trying to look like a human version of Barbie. She underwent more than 100 plastic surgeries. But just like you and me, she is aging.

When faced with the prospect of growing older, others have responded in different ways. "Age is mind over matter," joked the boxer Muhammad Ali. "As long as you don't mind, it doesn't matter."

Baseball Hall of Famer Joe DiMaggio admitted that when you get older, "You start chasing a ball, and your brain immediately commands your body, 'Run forward! Bend! Scoop up the ball! Peg it to the infield!' Then your body says, 'Who, me?'"

When asked what it's like to grow old, Babe Ruth put it bluntly: "It's hell to get older."

How about you? Would you agree with the Babe? Before you answer, consider for a minute some folks who paint an entirely different picture of the aging process. Although not on the level of Noah, who became the father of three after turning 500 and completed the ark 100 years later, many people refuse to act their age. Like the aging mosquito, they aren't content to wait for an opening—they get in there and make one. Here are just a few.

- At 75, Charles Schultz, the creator of the Peanuts comic strip, was still playing ice hockey.
- Leo Tolstoy learned to ride a bicycle at 67.
- Claude Monet began painting his famous Water Lily series at 76 and finished the work at 85.
- After 37 years out of the cockpit, aerobatic pilot Mary Victor Bruce flew a loop at 81.
- At 81, Cincinnati resident Harold Berkshire graduated from high school.
- At 82, William Ivy Baldwin became the oldest tightrope walker, crossing the South Boulder Canyon in Colorado on a 320-foot wire.

- Eamon de Valera was 90 when he served as president of Ireland.
- In his 90s, Albert Schweitzer ran a hospital in Africa.
- At 92, actor Kirk Douglas was blogging.
- At 94, Leopold Stokowski signed a six-year recording contract.
- At 70, Amos Alonzo Stagg retired as football coach at the University of Chicago and became coach of a small California college. He produced a winning team, was named Coach of the Year, and was still coaching advisor at age 98.
- At 91, George Bernard Shaw was still writing plays.
- At 100, Grandma Moses was still painting pictures.
- And Teiichi Igarishi celebrated his one hundredth birthday by climbing to the 12,395-foot summit of Mount Fuji.

I asked Gordon MacDonald, the author of numerous bestsellers, including *Ordering Your Private World,* what separates those who age gracefully from those who don't. Gordon told me that the elderly people he admires most share seven characteristics that have made their lives rich and kept them young.

1. They are thankful people. Their conversation and their correspondence are marked with appreciation.
2. They show enthusiastic interest in the accomplishments of the younger generation. Change is not their enemy, but their friend.
3. They keep their minds sharp and agile. Theirs is not the world of yesterday, but of today.
4. They are big-picture people. They look at life from the largest point of view, resisting panic when sudden events grab the headlines.

5. They never retire. They may slow down and walk away from a job, but they still live life with a mission.
6. They are servants. They realize that if people are going to see the show, others will have to be backstage.
7. They are not afraid of death. It's not that dying doesn't bother them, but they fully understand Paul's words in Philippians 1:21: "For to me, to live is Christ and to die is gain."

Since that meeting of the Circle of Six, I've done some reconsidering. And I've discovered that my idea of old age is changing. I used to think that life was lived on a hillside. That you went up, up, up until you reached about 50, at which point you hit an unavoidable banana peel and began a swift descent down the other side.

Paul's words make me wonder if I've had it backward. As we grow older, the things that matter in heaven should matter more on earth. As we age, the stuff of earth should lose its value.

Rich people are those who know that heaven is on the horizon and the best is yet to come. Maybe we've hit a banana peel, but there's cheesecake ahead.

I would not trade one moment of heaven for all the joys and riches of the world, even if it lasted for thousands and thousands of years.

MARTIN LUTHER

44

The Last Laugh

When our kids were small, Saturday night was pizza night at our house. If you had joined us, you'd find yourself sampling some of the finest pizza this side of Chicago. I should know. I made it. In my opinion, if this pizza were sold on the open market, it would cause the largest stampede since someone announced, "Thar's gold in them thar hills." My wife disagrees. She says this stuff would create the largest stampede since my mother started passing out cod liver oil pills. I'm quite sure she's joking. The kids seemed to like it. But they liked mud pies too.

Sometimes during the eating of my excellent pizza, we swarmed the living room to watch a video that was selected by the same method our forefathers used to select videos: a democratic vote. Since my wife and I are outnumbered, we have spent years watching cartoons. We have heard Bugs Bunny sing at the opera a hundred times. We have repeatedly witnessed the merciless shooting of Bambi's mother. We have seen Wile E. Coyote meet his Maker on countless occasions right in our living room. Lately I find myself cheering for the coyote. But the ending is always the same. He never fails to fail. You'd think he'd learn.

One night I talked the troops into watching *The Guns of Navarone.*

It's a little heavy on the suspense, but I thought it would be just fine. Halfway through I realized my mistake. I looked around me and saw children hiding everywhere—behind couches and chairs, holding pillows and blankets. I wondered if we should revisit the Road Runner.

Pushing the pause button, I said something that brought them out from behind their blockades. "Guys, you don't have to worry. I know the ending. The good guys lose."

"No...really?"

"I'm just kidding," I said. "But do you wanna know what happens?"

They wanted to know in the worst way. So I told them. The good guys win. It's as simple as that.

"Now do you wanna watch it?"

They did. In fact, soon they were dropping pillows and creeping out of their shelters. They eventually set aside their blankets and picked up the best pizza this side of Chicago. Even Ramona seemed to be enjoying it.

As a writer, I always look forward to opening my mail. But sometimes I wish I hadn't. Not long ago someone put my address at the top of a page and wrote these words below it:

> Dear Mr. Callaway,
>
> How can you write humor books when the world is falling apart? I think you need to get serious...We are in the last days here, and this is hardly a time for laughter.

I didn't quite know how to respond. In some respects the writer is right. We live in serious times. Like children sitting before the TV screen on a Saturday night, we're on pins and needles, wondering how a happy ending is possible. We read the papers, we watch the news, and we creep further and further behind our blockades.

Perhaps that's why I keep another letter handy, a letter I'll treasure for years to come. I've condensed it here for you:

> Dear Mr. Callaway,
>
> It's Tuesday today. Last Friday I visited my 85-year-old mother in the hospital. On my way to her room, I heard laughter. When I entered, I found Mom lying on the bed, surrounded by dozens of plastic tubes, a heart monitor, and a bedpan. She was reading one of your books and—despite her heart condition—laughing herself silly. Before I left, we spent some time talking about the hope we have as Christians and about heaven.
>
> Yesterday I received a phone call. Mom was with the Lord. It's been pretty tough, but I can't help thinking about the last time I saw Mom. I remember that she was laughing.

Sometimes I find myself pulling out that letter and reading it again. Sometimes I find myself thinking about an 85-year-old lady whom I can't wait to meet one day.

I'm sure that lying on that hospital bed, she wasn't thrilled with all that was going on around her. I'm sure that like me, she was concerned for her children. (And her grandchildren.) But still she could laugh. Why?

Because she knew the ending.

Her heavenly Father had told her of things to come. Of a better place. A place where her tears would be wiped dry, her health restored, and her question marks straightened into exclamation points. She knew that one day soon, she was heading home.

A friend of mine sells Steinway pianos and is often asked to play at funerals. One day he told me, "Phil, no one does funerals like followers of Jesus. There is no laughter...no real laughter...at anything but a Christian funeral."

Another friend was sitting by his son's bed one night. The boy, David, was dying of cancer. David took his dad's hand and said, "I need you to do something for me. Preach at my funeral. And talk about heaven, Dad."

His dad wiped the tears and nodded his head. How do you say no to that?

And his dad talked about heaven. Boy, did he ever. For about 20 minutes he expounded brilliantly on the promise of the resurrection and the joys of eternity with Jesus. Then he did a most unusual thing. Stepping away from the pulpit, he walked down the platform steps and stood in front of his son's open casket.

"David," he said, "We are far richer because you came into our lives, but now it's time to say goodnight. Goodnight, David. We love you." And with tears in his eyes, he gently closed the casket.

Then, turning to the audience, a beautiful smile stole across his face. "Goodnight…for now," he said. "But a good morning is on its way." With that, the song leader stood and started singing: "Soon and very soon, we are going to see the King!" And the congregation joined him. Throughout the church, tears gave way to laughter and sadness to rejoicing. In the face of death, celebration had broken out. Death had been swallowed up in victory.

One day soon, those of us who have put our trust in Jesus Christ will take part in that victory dance. One day soon those arms that were spread wide on a Roman cross will open once again and welcome us home to the richest life imaginable, a life that will never end.

So why should we not live every day as though it were our last? Why should we not take God's hand and walk bravely into the future? I do not have a ready answer for the suffering and brokenness and pain that touch us all. But I do know in the very depths of my being that one day we will have the last laugh. One day the tape will run out. The book will be closed, and all will be well.

"To live is Christ," wrote the apostle Paul. "To die is gain."

I guess you could say, "Live rich. Die richer."

Recommend virtue to your children; it alone, not money, can make them happy. I speak from experience.

Ludwig van Beethoven

45

Michael Jackson and Legacy

I almost fell asleep in the Country Music Hall of Fame. That's right. Twenty steps from Elvis Presley's gold-plated Cadillac, just around the corner from Webb Pierce's '62 Pontiac Bonneville convertible—the one with the seven-foot-wide pair of steer horns mounted on the front grille, pistols for door handles, and 150 silver dollars adorning the leather upholstery.

Blame my drowsiness on the theatre seats. They were a little too comfy. Blame my nodding head on the fact that I was tired—tired of hearing what fame has done to those who have slurped at its trough.

Ramona and I had just visited the featured exhibit "Family Tradition: Williams Family Legacy." "His is the standard by which success is measured in country music on every level, even self-destruction," a banner proclaimed, and I wanted to know more.

A rather frail and painfully introverted man, Hank was known as much for his legend as his music. He rose to fame in the fall of 1947 with his hit "Move It on Over" and then moved it on to Nashville in June 1949, swiftly becoming one of the brightest stars in country music. Before long his song "Hey, Good Lookin'" graced the pop charts, and the accolades and money poured in.

But Hank drank too much. So much in fact, that in 1952, his wife Audrey ordered him out of the family home. As 1952 wore on, Hank's appearances dwindled, and in August his drunkenness became such a serious problem that he was fired by the Grand Ole Opry. In October, when he married again, another girlfriend was pregnant with his child. Though his song "Jambalaya" rose to number one, Hank could find no peace. On December 30 he left for two bookings in Charleston, West Virginia, and Canton, Ohio. He died in the backseat of his chauffeured Cadillac and was pronounced dead New Year's Day, 1953, in Oak Hill, West Virginia.

He was 29.

As I read of his life, I couldn't help thinking about the word *legacy.* Simply put, it's a baton. It's what we pass along in this race to those who come behind.

I was climbing off a plane on June 25, 2009 when my cell phone vibrated. I had been in Toronto at a celebration of the ministry of Charles Swindoll, and Ramona told me that things were fine at home, that she couldn't wait to see me, and, oh yes, that Michael Jackson had died.

I asked her when, and it turned out that while I was sharing a stage with Mr. Swindoll talking to leaders about integrity and legacy, a doctor in Los Angeles was trying to resuscitate the talented and troubled King of Pop.

You could hardly turn on a radio when I was in high school without bumping into a Michael Jackson song. Or go out in public without seeing someone attempt the moonwalk. Michael was unarguably one of the most gifted performers of all time (try moonwalking without hurting something), and I don't believe anyone is created to deal with fame on the scale he was. But since his death, whenever I think about his life, sadness hits me hard. Though his album sales were nearing a billion copies at his death, acquaintances and friends repeatedly describe his deep sadness. One called him "the loneliest man I ever knew." The *New York Post* estimated that he left behind a debt of $500 million. He also left an estranged family and a string of broken relationships.

Once again I was thinking about that word: *legacy.*

Manfred Kets de Vries provides some insight into the reason the average celebrity lives 20 years less than the guy who works in a coal mine. Manfred is one of a new breed of therapists who treat angst among the outrageously rich. When Saudi Arabia's Prince Alwaleed bin Talal purchased a new Airbus A380 Superjumbo as his private jet, Manfred observed, "For the superrich, houses, yachts, cars and planes are like new toys that they play with for five minutes and then lose interest in...All the spending is a mad attempt to cover up boredom and depression."

According to de Vries, the superrich succumb to a little something he dubs Wealth Fatigue Syndrome. When money is available in nearly limitless quantities, the victim sinks into a kind of inertia. Feeling any sort of excitement means taking more and more risks, financially and physically. Luxury holidays are replaced by rappelling in Australia and swimming with sharks. The first-class ticket of old becomes a private jet and then a Superjumbo like Alwaleed's. The quest for more pleasure means later nights and bigger parties. Drugs are abused to sleep, to awake, and to perform. Regardless of how much money is banked, it never satisfies. It's as useless as fishing in a parking lot.

Celebrity Moby has a wall of gold and platinum disks—and has been in therapy for substance abuse. He told the *Guardian* (London), "The people buying the celebrity magazines are miserable because they see Puff Daddy and Jessica Simpson on a yacht in St. Bart's and think it's a fantastic life. It's not. It's a depressing life. They're not attractive in reality because they spend hours with stylists making them attractive."

On June 25, 2009 I determined to spend more time celebrating and savoring the legacies of those who don't have as much time for the stylists because they've been too busy pointing me in the right direction.

Hebrews 13:7 instructs us, "Remember your leaders, who spoke the word of God to you. Consider the outcome of their way of life and imitate their faith."

I think of people like Chuck Swindoll, who showed me how to

draw people with humor so they can hear the truth. People like my mother, who taught me to look on the needs of others and seek Jesus above all. I think of unheralded housewives and ordained plumbers who go about their daily tasks with joy, passing the baton on to their children, whom they love and pray for.

My father left many books behind, and as I've read them, they've become part of his legacy to me. One is a hand-signed copy of a book by the old fiery preacher Vance Havner. In it I found a quote from Babe Ruth, who spoke of a humble minister he had known. "I've signed my name on hundreds of baseballs. He wrote his on human hearts. I am called a great home run [hitter], but compared to him, I didn't make first base."

A few years ago movie star Denzel Washington was up for an Academy Award. A self-professing follower of Jesus, Denzel was bothered by the politics of it all and worried about the possible outcome. His mother spoke liberating words that made him smile, "Just remember, man gives the award, but God gives the reward."

Denzel told the story to a reporter and then added, "As long as I please him, then I'm pleased."

One of the primary goals of life is to prepare for the end of it. To hear God's welcome greeting, "Well done, good and faithful servant." To discover with the millions who have gone before that the rewards for a lasting legacy are out of this world.

Let us so live that when we come to die
even the undertaker will be sorry.

Mark Twain

46

When I Hang Up My Sneakers

Just this morning someone kindly notified me that I am dead. According to a fourth grader who wrote a story on me for an assignment, I was born in 1996 and died at the age of ten. I shall protect her name, but I certify her report entirely fact free, which reminds me of many of my own assignments throughout elementary school. Here is part of her report: "My report is about Phil Callaway because he is a great writer. He can always make me laugh no matter what for. I especially liked *Laughing Matters.* It is very funny. He writes humorous writing because he loves to be funny. He is a dad with two of his kids. They are both girls."

As Mark Twain wrote, "The reports of my death are greatly exaggerated." But the truth is, I did have my annual physical last week. Doctor Dan probed and prodded and poked. Then he shook his head. "Well, Phil," he mused with a concerned look on his face, "I give you about 37 years to live." I told him he had nearly given me a heart attack and the only way he could make it up to me was with a pocketful of free samples.

Now that I have officially reached the age where candles on my birthday cake have been replaced by a giant sparkler and sprinkler heads, it's time to shop for epitaphs. Believe me, there are some pretty funny tombstones out there. Here are my favorites, some corny, some clever:

- "See? I told you I was sick!"

- "I was afraid this would happen."
- "Here lies an atheist, all dressed up and no place to go."
- "Here lies the body of Jonathan Blake. Stepped on the gas instead of the brake."
- "Here lies John Yeast. Pardon me for not rising."
- In Hollywood Forever Cemetery is the tombstone of Mel Blanc, the man of a thousand voices, including Bugs Bunny, Daffy Duck, and Porky Pig. It reads, "That's All, Folks."
- "Here lies Ezekial Aikle, age 102. The good die young."
- "Here lies a man named Zeke, second-fastest draw in Cripple Creek."
- "Jonathan Thompson. A pious Christian and affectionate husband. His disconsolate widow continues to carry on his grocery business on Main Street. Cheapest and best prices in town."
- "Let your wind blow free where'er you may be. Holding it in was the death of me."

In Enosburg, Vermont, an inscription over the grave of Anna Hopewill reads, "Here lies the body of beloved Anna, done to death by a fresh banana. It wasn't the fruit that laid her low, but the skin of the thing that made her go."

In Pembroke, Massachusetts, a weary homemaker lies below these words: "Everything here is exact to my wishes. Because no one eats, there is no washing of dishes."

An English lawyer by the name of John Strange had this pun etched on his headstone: "Here lies an honest lawyer, and that is Strange."

The grave marker of a couple from Prescott, Massachusetts, also reveals a great deal about their marriage: "Here lies the body of Obadiah Wilkinson and his wife, Ruth. Their warfare is accomplished."

A woman in Key West, Florida, was married to a man who was known for his unfaithfulness, so she ordered a tombstone that read, "Frank, at least I know where you're sleeping tonight." So many tourists chipped away pieces of the headstone as souvenirs that she was forced to replace it without the biting commentary.

How about you? What would you like on your tombstone? One lady said, "I will just die if nobody comes to my funeral!"

Let's face it, most of us would like to be remembered by someone. And what will they remember? I have posed a question to hundreds of the best-known Christians of our time: "How would you like to be remembered?" I think you'll enjoy their answers.

Robin Mark, who penned the well-loved song "These Are the Days of Elijah," responded, "My staggering good looks and finely crafted athleticism! Or failing that, I'd like to be remembered by my children as a good father. That may sound cheesy, but it's so important to me."

Here's the reply of Jim Cymbala, pastor of the famed Brooklyn Tabernacle:

> I don't care to be remembered. There was an old saying among the holiness camps of the 1800s and early 1900s that you knew it had been a good meeting when people went home and didn't talk about who preached. In other words, if they talked about how clever the preacher was or his skills as an orator, you knew the meeting wasn't very good. But when people went home saying, "Isn't Jesus wonderful?" you knew the speaker had allowed God to take center stage. I'd be happy not to be remembered at all if I knew I had influenced someone to serve the Lord.

Josh McDowell, author and internationally renowned apologist said, "I'd like to be remembered as a man who was obedient and faithful right up to the end. I want to take as many people as I can with me to heaven and enjoy life along the way." Sixteen years later while talking with Josh, I asked if his answer had changed. He said, "No. I want my legacy to be people, not buildings. I'm not concerned about leaving a big legacy. I'm concerned about being faithful. And then if I can challenge others to love the Lord with all their heart, mind, and soul, my life is complete."

Popular singer Rebecca St. James answered, "I'd like to be remembered as a woman who passionately loved God and people."

St. Louis Cardinals MVP first baseman Albert Pujols responded this way: "You know how I want people to remember me? I don't want to be remembered as the best baseball player ever. I want to be remembered as a great guy who loved the Lord, who loved to serve the community, and who gave back." My wife and I spent time at a project in the Dominican Republic where Pujols and his wife sponsor 50 teenage mothers, paying for their education, medicine, and food through a church.

Elisabeth Elliot, whose husband Jim Elliot (famous for the words "He is no fool who gives what he cannot keep to gain what he cannot lose") was killed by Auca Indians in South America, had a simple answer: "I want to be remembered as a servant of God. Nothing else."

Singer/songwriter Michael Card, best known for his song "El Shaddai," responded this way:

> My flesh says I want to be remembered as some great songwriter, but before every concert I've prayed, "Lord, hide me in Yourself. Don't let me be seen; let Christ be seen." So I don't particularly care to be remembered. I would like my wife and kids to remember me as someone who loved them and cared more about them than myself. But beyond that I don't care to be remembered, because I've tried to point people to Christ.

Steve Green, another popular singer, recalled the words of R.A. Torrey: "You can't tell the effectiveness of a man's ministry until you see the lives of his grandchildren." Then he added, "After I am gone, I pray that my children and grandchildren will be able to say that Steve Green was an example to them of faithfulness to God. That in spite of past wanderings, my goal was to glorify him."

Evangelist Luis Palau, who has spoken to hundreds of millions through his radio and television broadcasts, would like to be remembered "as someone who was faithful to Scripture. Someone who never ceased to preach the gospel of Jesus Christ to as many people as possible. That's what I love to do—faithfully present the gospel."

Rick Warren put it this way, "My life verse is Acts 13:36, the short phrase that says, 'David served God's purpose in his generation, then he died.' He served God's purpose—that's eternal. In his generation—he did it in a contemporary way. He did the timeless in a timely way. He did that which never changes in a world that's always changing. I can't think of a better epitaph than that I served God's purpose and then died. That's what we're here for."

Songwriter and singer Twila Paris, who wrote the popular hymn "He Is Exalted," said this:

> My father, my grandfather, and my great-grandfather were ministers, and I believe that many of the blessings I experience in my life and ministry are a result of the faithfulness of people I've never met. That makes me want to leave a legacy of faithfulness. After I'm gone, I hope that some young person who doesn't even know my name will be influenced toward the truth and the uncompromising position that Jesus called us to because I was a thread and a link in the body of Christ—because I was faithful.

Country music star Paul Brandt said, "For a long time I thought that a legacy was about having your name on a room at the Children's Hospital or being remembered for the money you raised for some great cause. But the legacy of all Christians should be that they pointed people to the Lord. That's how I want to be remembered."

Steven Curtis Chapman said, "I would like my wife to say, 'I saw his failures. I saw him blow it, but his greatest desire was to live a life that honored Jesus Christ.' I hope my children will say I was a committed father. And it would be nice if people remembered a song here and there, but that's pretty insignificant compared to my desire to know Christ and to make him known."

Michael W. Smith said, "I've never been asked that before. I guess

I would love if my tombstone would say, 'He loved well, and he was a great husband and a great father.'"

When Max Lucado, one of the bestselling authors of our time, was in high school, he developed a drinking problem.

> The definition for drunk is vague, but it would take me six beers to feel the buzz. I came from a family of alcoholics, and I don't even like to think about all the messes I would have made by now had not Christ intervened. But in the end, I hope it will be said that I showed the splendor of God, that I showed why he is worthy of worship. That's what matters. Of course, I think I would feel like a failure if my children didn't remember me as a good father too. That's what keeps me going. That and trying to break 90 on the golf course.

Nine years later, I asked Max the same question. He smiled again. "Well, I gave up on the last one," he laughed. "But I'd say the same today. If it's God's will, I'd like to continue to write for the rest of my life, but the things that pushes my button the most are my daughters. I really love them."

Author, speaker, and sociologist Tony Campolo said, "When I hang up my sneakers, I pray there will be hundreds of kids on the mission field because I helped them feel a passion for those who didn't know Jesus."

And popular songwriter Gloria Gaither, whose song "Because He Lives" has been translated into almost every known language on earth, summed it up this way: "If I had to write my epitaph, it would probably say, 'She gave herself away for the things that last forever.'"

And what would I like on my tombstone? Simply this: "He found God's grace too amazing to keep to himself."

It won't make people laugh or be chipped away as a souvenir. But if it speaks of a life lived for God, graced by friendships, and nourished by joy and hope, then I will have lived the richest life of all.

Epilogue

Each time I conspire to lay a book to rest, life happens. My computer crashes. My car gets slammed into in a Walmart parking lot. Someone tries to charge $5600 on my MasterCard (no, it was not my wife).

This time it had to do with my mother. And with money.

When my father was my age, he owned a life insurance policy worth $25,000. Anything else was a luxury. The house was a rental. The car was a wreck. He had no investments. No savings account. No guarantees. In fact, when he found out how much I ate, Dad cashed in that insurance policy to pay the bills.

Mom loved to tell of the time Dad offered to open a joint savings account with her. She declined. "I'd rather open it with someone who has money," she laughed. Then she would grow very serious. "God has supplied all our needs at every turn of the road."

Early in their marriage, Dad turned down a high-paying job so he could enter the ministry. I don't think they had a clue how lean the years would be. And I'm sure they had their moments of regretting his decision, moments of worrying about their retirement plan. Would God really come through?

As they moved into their seventies, a secure future seemed out of the question. Their health was on the decline. Their worries were on the rise.

No longer able to look after a three-bedroom house, they began shuffling through retirement homes, trying to ask the right questions.

One spring morning, as Ramona and I flipped through house plans, she caught me off guard. "Why don't we put a suite in this house we're building?" she asked. "Your parents could live there."

A dozen mother-in-law jokes came to mind, but Ramona wasn't kidding. "They've been so good to us," she said. "If we can do it, I think we should."

"Would we put thick metal locks on the doors?" I asked with a grin. She said it was no problem. "Would we make it super soundproof?" She said we would. "How about an alarm system? Maybe a guard dog?" She said I was pushing it.

Over coffee and ice cream, we told Mom and Dad of our plans. I don't think I'd seen Dad so happy since he had his corns removed. They were overwhelmed. Tears spilled down both their faces. "Thank you," they kept saying.

For five years, they graced that suite with their presence. "The happiest years of our lives," they often said. And almost every night along about bedtime, the kids disappeared. We didn't have to look far. Rachael would be cuddled on the couch, studying the lines on Grandma's hands. Stephen was usually flat out on the carpet, throwing something breakable in the air. One blustery evening I heard Jeffrey reading them a bedtime story—the story of Abraham, who followed God into an uncertain future.

Like the old patriarch, Mom and Dad had done this too. Moving a few thousand miles from home, they tested God's promise: "No good thing will he withhold from them that walk uprightly." And they found it to be true.

Time marches along. A few years ago I lost my dad (though I'm quick to remind myself that you haven't lost someone when you know exactly where he is). And the very day this book was due, my mother passed into the presence of Jesus. Safe at home. Freedom 85.

Mom and Dad didn't leave much behind. Believe me, we've looked.

Or did they?

A few years back, each of us children picked out something from their small cache of earthly stuff. Dan selected a living room set. Ruth, some jewelry. Too bad for my brother Tim—he went with their car, which lasted a month. I chose an object that sat on their mantel for three decades. It was a twenty-fifth anniversary gift they first got when I was five. I always loved that clock—opening the back of it, winding it up, watching the Westminster chimes. That clock called me for breakfast and tortured me at bedtime. It crawled along during piano practice and sped up on weekends. And I suppose, in some small way, it made me mindful that no matter what, time keeps ticking. That we should make the most of what's left.

The clock sits on my mantle now. It's the best inheritance a kid could wish for because it reminds me of my parents' lives. Lives of faithfulness to each other. Lives of service to God. Lives rich in texture and brimming with hope.

My prayer as you close this book is that you will live that way. May you slow down enough to listen to God's voice, remember daily the things that last, and chase only the eternal.

Like that clock, may this book serve as a small reminder of the things that matter most. A reminder that the simple things in life are the best things. That friendship, peace, joy, and hope are worth pursuing. And that they just may be closer than we think.

I'd love to hear from you. When you have a few minutes, drop me a note and tell me what has made your life rich. Meanwhile, visit me online at laughagain.org for a complimentary study guide. Until then, may God bless you. Richly.

Phil Callaway
PO Box 514
Three Hills, AB Canada
T0M 2A0

Notes

Preface: Poor Little Rich Boy

1. Keith Hinson, "Inheritance Windfall May Bypass Churches," *Christianity Today,* April 7, 1997, 58. According to a Cornell Department of Economics and Housing study reported in the New York Times, the richest 1 percent of the population stand to each receive an average inheritance of $3.6 million; the next richest 9 percent are dividing another third for an average inheritance of about $396,000; the remaining 90 percent will share the rest. That means an average inheritance of about $40,000 for this group.

Part One: Rich People Know the Speed Limit

1. Ellen Vaughn, *Time Peace* (Grand Rapids, MI: Zondervan, 2007), 69. Ellen's book is one of the finest on the topic of time and eternity you will ever read.
2. Mark Aguiar and Erik Hurst, "Measuring Trends in Leisure: The Allocation of Time over Five Decades," National Bureau of Economic Research, Working Paper no. 12082, March 2006, 14-16. Available online at www.nber.org/papers/W12082.
3. Doctors are now treating Wii-related injuries. Researchers at Leeds Teaching Hospital have even identified an injury they called "Wii knee." They fear "an epidemic."
4. Fareed Zakaria, *The Post-American World* (New York: Norton, 2009), 133.
5. Gene Weingarten, "Pearls Before Breakfast," *Washington Post,* Sunday, April 8, 2007.
6. "Americans Ditching Urban Jungles for Greener Pastures," Associated Press, March 4, 2007.
7. I did not make up her name.
8. Richard Smith, "Lottery couple Claire Owen and Craig Pope split after winning £5 million jackpot," *Mirror.co.uk News,* May 29, 2008.
9. Nancy Gibbs, "The Great Recession: American Becomes Thrift Nation," *Time,* April 15, 2009, 22. In the space of one month, *Time* featured these two cover stories: "The End of Excess" and "The New Frugality." Both echoed the wise advice from sages of an earlier age: When you spend what you don't have, something has to give.
10. Vikas Bajaj, "Equity Loans as Next Round in Credit Crisis," *New York Times,* March 27, 2008. Available online at www.nytimes.com/2008/03/27/business/27loan.html.

Part Two: Rich People Hit Curveballs

1. Psalm 46:1.
2. Jeremiah 29:11.
3. A friend suggested an easy solution to the deer problem. Every time you cut your hair, wrap it in pantyhose and hang a little from the tree. It works. Really. The deer avoid the tree. And eat your shrubs.

Part Three: Rich People Are People People

1. "Massive diamond found in Lesotho," BBC News, September 21, 2008. Available online at news.bbc.co.uk/2/hi/africa/7628475.stm.
2. Called "Acres of Diamonds," this story was originally told by Dr. Russell Herman Conwell (1843–1925), who traveled the United States, repeating it an estimated six thousand times. The story attracted the attention of literally millions of people, and the money raised from Dr. Conwell's lectures—totaling $6 million—was used to found Temple University in Philadelphia, bringing to reality his dream of building a first-class university for poor but deserving youth.
3. So many people have written and stopped me on the street to ask me if this is true that we have posted pictures at www.laughagain.org. We have not tampered with these pictures, they are the real thing. I cannot lie about any of these details. Believe me, there are too many witnesses.
4. I heard this from other players often. And from their parents. Once a lady waited for me and chased me to the parking lot wielding a whiskey bottle. I earned $12 refereeing that game and soon decided to try another line of work.

Part Four: Rich People Know Where the Buck Stops

1. If you're reading this, Will, allow me to say that I was wrong and I am sorry and I certainly hope things are going very well for you, so well that you have plenty of suspects to prosecute without thinking of your dear old friend. PS: I *never* laugh at lawyer jokes. No sir, not me. I didn't even get the one about the busload of lawyers going over a cliff.
2. Ninety-two percent who responded to this survey live in North America. The most unanticipated item to me was the camera. Each time it was mentioned, the word *memories* was used in the same sentence.
3. James 4:14.
4. 1 Timothy 6:17.
5. Which I happen to be selling on my website.

Part Five: Rich People Leave the Right Stuff Behind

1. Several years after high school, my friend and his new bride were walking around a mall 1000 miles from home, and they happened to meet this former teacher. They stopped to talk with him, but all he said was "Hi, May 3," and then he walked away. Needless to say, this dear soul's elevator wasn't stopping at all the right floors, and I can't remember a thing I learned from him. But I never forget my friend's birthday.

2. Adapted from Terry C. Muck, *Those Other Religions in Your Neighborhood* (Grand Rapids: Zondervan, 1992), 150-51.
3. I also wonder why there were no global warming conferences in Canada during the month of January, and why the Canadian scientists studying these things all winter in Phoenix.
4. The bulk of this chapter is from a recorded interview with Carl Medearis, author of the fabulous book *Muslims, Christians, and Jesus* (Bloomington, MN: Bethany House), 2009.
5. Michael Sherrod and Matthew Rayback, *Bad Baby Names* (Ancestry.com, 2008).
6. Whom we named after two Bible characters—Moses, who stuttered, and Jonah, who ran away.
7. It took me years to discover that many of my mother's statements had been stolen from the Bible. I later found this one in Psalm 127:1.

About the Author

Phil Callaway is the bestselling author of more than 20 books and a popular speaker for conferences, churches, and corporations. His books, including *Laughing Matters, Golfing with the Master, Who Put My Life on Fast-Forward,* and *Family Squeeze,* have been translated into languages like Chinese, Korean, Spanish, and English—one of which he speaks fluently. His five-part video series *The Big Picture* has been viewed in 80,000 churches worldwide. Phil is married to his high school sweetheart, Ramona, and is president of a fan club for each of their three grown children. For more information on his books, DVDs, or Phil's speaking ministry, visit www.laughagain.org, e-mail him at callaway@prairie.edu, or write him at

PO Box 514
Three Hills, AB Canada
T0M 2A0

Make Your Life Richer Without Any Money

Phil is editor of *Servant* magazine, an award-winning magazine read in more than 100 countries. A ministry of Prairie Bible Institute, *Servant* is full of insightful interviews, helpful articles, and Phil's good humor. For a complimentary one-year subscription, please call 1-800-221-8532, email servant@prairie.edu, or write to

Servant Magazine
PO Box 4000
Three Hills, AB
T0M 2N0